An insightful book, eloquently arguing for w
– but sadly is often not – which is that gre;
great engagement skills. CEOs are now also chief repuauon uiii.i
for the organizations that they have the privilege to lead. Charlotte
Otter's tightly written analysis gives new currency to this old idea,
highlighting the urgency of prevention rather than cure (or 'vitamins
rather than aspirins' in Otter's words) when it comes to building
and protecting the perceptions that matter. Her call for new more
neuro-diverse leaders to step up is urgent, powerful and timely. This
book, jam-packed with great stories from interviews with over 40
people from different backgrounds, shows how leaders can reshape
themselves in practice. It is a must read for the marzipan layer of
emerging talent who are considering if they have what it takes to
make the leadership leap.

Rupert Younger, Director, Oxford University
Centre for Corporate Reputation

This book double clicks on a range of critical leadership topics and
is enriched with real voices from diverse perspectives. As a chief
communications officer, I know that trust and credibility are built
over years and potentially destroyed in minutes. With increasing
geoeconomic complexity, navigating this has never been more
'interesting'. *We Need New Leaders* offers so many insights of value
to any aspiring leader, but particularly for those looking to deepen
their craft as a communications professional. How refreshing to
read that authenticity and a focus on inclusion are valued leadership
superpowers.

Lynette Jackson, Chief Communications Officer, Siemens

We Need New Leaders is a compelling call to action for a new
generation of leaders who understand that navigating today's
complex landscape requires more than just competence – it
demands authenticity, empathy and the ability to build trust through

consistent, meaningful actions. Charlotte Otter's insights on how reputation shapes leadership success provide a powerful guide for anyone looking to lead with purpose and impact. A must-read for aspiring leaders and those seeking to redefine the status quo in the C-Suite.

Frank Wolf, Co-Founder and Chief Strategy Officer Staffbase, Author of *The Narrative Age*

Careers are built on a strong reputation, and safeguarding it is far too important to be left to chance. *We Need New Leaders* provides valuable insights to every leader on how to actively manage their reputation by working closely with the communication team.

Hala Zeine, Chief Strategy Officer, ServiceNow

In today's dynamic business environment, reputation isn't just a corporate asset – it's a leader's legacy. *We Need New Leaders* dives into the vital partnership between CEOs and CCOs, highlighting how this collaboration shapes organizational resilience and reputation. As someone passionate about human-centred leadership and strategic communication, I found the insights on the CEO–CCO relationship and its unique 'truth to power' dynamic incredibly relevant for modern leaders.

For those navigating the complexities of corporate reputation – especially leaders from diverse backgrounds facing unique challenges – Charlotte Otter's book offers a thoughtful lens and actionable takeaways. A must-read for anyone committed to building trust and fostering influence in the C-Suite!

Monique Zytnik, Author of *Internal Communication in the Age of Artificial Intelligence*, Communication Strategist, and IABC EMENA Region Chair

Never has a book been more needed. In an age where we risk allowing those who shout loudest to get the largest rewards Charlotte Otter has provided a deeply researched and eminently practical treatise that both questions that fact and provides a way forward. While we might never put the 'loudmouth leadership genie' back in the bottle this book shows those who are subjected to it how they can question what is happening, and those who may be tempted down that road how to build authentic and sustainable engagement built on values driven trust. It's a book that could change the world one leader at a time.

David Pullan, Author of *The DNA of Engagement*

In a world grappling with declining trust in leadership, *We Need New Leaders* emerges as a timely and vital guiding tool. In her book, Charlotte Otter masterfully blends insightful analysis with practical strategies, offering a much-needed roadmap for a diverse pool of aspiring CEOs. Drawing upon original research and numerous interviews, Otter illuminates the unique challenges faced by leaders from underrepresented backgrounds – challenges that often extend beyond competence and into the realm of reputation. An inspiring read, the book's strength lies in its concise, actionable advice on building authentic reputations, fostering crucial relationships with communications teams, and navigating the complexities of modern leadership in a highly-charged environment.

We Need New Leaders is not just a handbook; it's a crucial manifesto for change. It's a must-read for aspiring CEOs from diverse backgrounds, seasoned executives seeking to build more inclusive teams, and communications professionals working to create a more equitable and trustworthy leadership landscape. This book is a powerful tool for progress, and an essential guide, showing aspiring CEOs how to leverage reputation management to achieve and maintain top leadership roles.

Nthabiseng Makgatho, Brand Marketing
Expert and Owner of Blinq Consulting

Reputation is an intangible asset for companies and for leaders. *We Need New Leaders* sets out a compelling manifesto and a path for leaders from diverse backgrounds – who face systemic and structural obstacles to leadership success and want to make a tangible difference to their companies, and their societies. Based on recent research as well as her experience leading executive communications at a global technology company, Charlotte Otter makes the case for leaders who are outside the norm to partner with their communication directors and teams. This cogent and timely book is a useful companion for leaders looking to build their reputations and secure career success.

Kathy Harvey, Associate Dean, Degree Programmes, Oxford Said Business School, NED and Board member

We Need New Leaders clearly highlights how reputation equity can help to break down systemic barriers for founders and CEOs from diverse backgrounds. You don't often find a book on leadership communication that contains an entire chapter on communicating as a founder. I really enjoyed the combination of practical strategies and compelling insights in Charlotte Otter's well-written and powerful book.

Dr Larissa Leitner, Co-Founder and MD of Empion

Distilling years of experience in her own role as a comms director at a global IT business, Charlotte makes the case for business leaders that are well, more like us. By that I mean developing a pipeline of leaders who reflect the rich diversity of people across our communities.

Marc Thompson, Senior Fellow Strategy and Organisation, Oxford University

The best time to learn how to be a great leader is before you start leading; the next best time is now, with this book. Charlotte Otter's in-depth research and interviews with business leaders has resulted in this generous, indispensable volume on reputation building for current and future leaders.

Linda Sidzumo-Dietel, Digital Transformation Senior Manager, International Baccalaureate Organization

We Need New Leaders is a powerful call to action for fostering equity in entrepreneurship and corporate spaces. Highlighting the structural barriers faced by founders and CEOs with diverse identities, it offers practical strategies for building reputation equity, grounded in authenticity and meaningful connections.

Rosie Ginday MBE, CEO and Founder, Miss Macaroon

Achieving a diverse and resilient generation of leaders is essential for organizations navigating the realities of a complex world. Sustaining the success of leaders from diverse backgrounds calls for something more: an intentional effort to build trust both within and beyond their organizations. Building that trust is a collaborative process.

A champion for the power of authentic communications to help organizations and their leaders thrive, Charlotte Otter uses real-world stories to show emerging leaders how a trusted partnership with their senior communications officer can help them to build their reputation and confidence as an effective leader. *We Need New Leaders* makes the latest research and ideas about the future of leadership accessible, actionable, and personal.

Tara Montgomery, Leadership Coach and Founder/Principal, Civic Health Partners

Charlotte Otter's *We Need New Leaders* really resonated with me. Even in the 21st century, we find able-bodied men of the majority race getting an easier time when pursuing a leadership role, while unreasonable expectations and judgements are levelled at anyone outside this archetype. We are also being limited by the paternalistic, bureaucratic ways we work. This book helps us rethink the system, with inspiring, real-world examples of people who have done just that, showing us that leadership can be inclusive, authentic, even vulnerable – and, most of all, human. Intelligently and thoroughly researched, Charlotte shows that there is no single mould of leader, and why going against the archetype can work effectively for organizations. She provides a practical toolkit on how new leadership models can create new strengths, and her way of considering reputation equity helps us rethink what makes a truly strong organization that is united in its goals and purpose.

Jack Yan, CEO Jack Yan & Associates,
Co-Chair Medinge Group

In the age of AI, reputation management has become more critical than ever, and this starts with the reputation of the leader. *We Need New Leaders* provides invaluable, research-backed industry insights and pragmatic advice for emerging and established leaders on how to develop their own reputation building blocks using strategic communications and effective stakeholder engagement.

Katja Schroeder, Senior Lecturer, School of
Professional Studies, Columbia University

Charlotte Otter's *We Need New Leaders* is more than just a book; it's a rallying cry for anyone ready to build leadership based on equity, empathy and engagement. In our ever-changing world, Charlotte boldly argues for a new kind of leadership that meets today's challenges head-on. With her extensive background in reputation management and leadership transformation, she shows us why diversity, inclusion and a strong sense of leadership identity are essential. The book is filled with real-life stories, research and insights from various leaders, making it both inspiring and practical. Whether you're a leader looking to evolve, a communicator shaping essential conversations, or someone who wants to drive meaningful change, Charlotte provides the tools you need.

Advita Patel, CEO and Founder CommsRebel,
Communications and Inclusion Strategist

In a world that actively seeks authentic leaders who reflect the diverse fabric of our global community, Charlotte Otter's *We Need New Leaders* emerges as a symbol of hope. This book effectively underscores the urgent need for leaders who represent our society's myriad backgrounds, ethnicities and cultures.

Charlotte's insightful analysis of reputation management provides a valuable framework for aspiring leaders who wish to cultivate trust and navigate the complexities of leadership. Her emphasis on the interplay of character, coherence and competence is crucial for anyone aspiring to create a lasting impact.

Vikas Goel, Director, Shiker Consulting

We are living in unprecedented times, confronting challenges that are both urgent and complex. Now more than ever, from business to non-profit and especially in government, *We Need New Leaders*. This book offers a transformative and essential guide for new and emerging leaders.

Charlotte illustrates how words matter – leadership is not just about action but how we communicate those actions. Recognizing the systemic hurdles that diverse leaders face in their journeys, this book serves as a dynamic tool to help navigate the many obstacles along the way. Emerging leaders will explore how to weave together effective communication with an authentic sense of self in order to inspire change, build trust and create long-lasting impact.

Aparna Bhasin, Founder, Coach and Facilitator,
Aparna Bhasin Consulting

From her experience in the front lines of leadership at an international Fortune 500 company, research on communications approaches and theory, and through candid interviews with a diverse set of communications leaders, Charlotte Otter provides a thorough and compelling analysis of the change that we need to see in leaders. Her exploration of how leaders can move away from toxic, unhealthy practices and can bring their whole selves to work and embrace authenticity and their identities is refreshing. I only wish I could have read this decades ago when embarking on my own leadership journey.

Daniel Atlin, Strategy Consulting and
Executive Coach, DJA Sensemaking

In today's world dominated by social media, reputation is everything. And managing reputation – the intersection between how you show up and how you talk about it – is critical for any leader, senior or aspiring. But this cannot be done without understanding its mechanics. Drawing from over 40 interviews with leaders from diverse backgrounds, Charlotte helps us recognize patterns in individuals who have managed reputation proactively to keep and land top jobs.

We Need New Leaders is an invaluable resource for any CEO or founder, especially if you do not fit the archetypical mold. At the end of the day, reputation is all about perception, and it's only leaders who look like the traditional leadership norm that have the privilege of not thinking about it.

Amanda Nolen, Advisor, Investor, NED

we need new
LEADERS

Mastering reputation management to reshape the C-Suite

Charlotte Otter

First published in Great Britain by Practical Inspiration Publishing, 2025

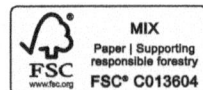

ISBN   9781788607629   (hardback)
       9781788607636   (paperback)
       9781788607643   (epub)
       9781788607650   (Kindle)

EU GPSR representative: LOGOS EUROPE, 9 rue Nicolas Poussin, LA ROCHELLE 17000, France Contact@logoseurope.eu

Want to bulk-buy copies of this book for your team and colleagues? We can customize the content and co-brand *We Need New Leaders* to suit your business's needs.

Please email info@practicalinspiration.com for more details.

Practical Inspiration Publishing™

MIX
Paper | Supporting responsible forestry
FSC
www.fsc.org   FSC® C013604

Also by Charlotte Otter

Balthasar's Gift
Karkloof Blue

Contents

Foreword .... *xv*
Notes for the reader .... *xix*

Introduction 1

Part 1 New leadership priorities
1   The leadership crisis 11
2   Diversity still matters...23
3   Finding the leader within – landing or creating a
     dream job 41
4   Finding the right culture – keeping a dream job 57

Part 2 New relationship metrics
5   Understanding reputation 75
6   Understanding corporate versus CEO reputation.................87
7   Reputational risk and crisis management............................101
8   Building a relationship to manage reputation.....................115

Part 3 New reputation equity
9   Creating your reputation equity...133
10   Reputation equity for non-CEOs...147
11   Reputation equity for founders – when you're both
     CEO and CCO...167
12   Towards new leaders..179

Acknowledgements 189
Resources... 191
Notes 195
Bibliography.. 203
Index 207

Foreword

In today's hyper-connected world, reputation is a currency as valuable as revenue. A single tweet, a fleeting headline or even the absence of a timely response can ripple through markets, stakeholders and public opinion. For leaders navigating these turbulent waters, mastering executive presence is not just a skill but a critical business imperative. It is in this context that this book holds its significance, shedding light on the transformative power of effective communication and the profound partnership between a CEO and their Communications Officer.

Having had the privilege of leading in dynamic environments, I have witnessed firsthand how corporate identity shapes not only the perception of an organization but also its ability to innovate, grow and lead. It is often said that 'reputation arrives on foot but leaves on horseback.' This is a stark reminder that building trust is a painstaking process, yet it can be undone in an instant. The ability to protect and enhance credibility requires more than just damage control; it demands foresight, authenticity and a deeply ingrained culture of transparency and accountability.

At the heart of this effort lies a unique and indispensable partnership: the bond between the CEO and their Communications Officer. This relationship is one of mutual trust, where the Communications Officer is both a strategist and a confidant, offering a clear-eyed perspective on how decisions resonate beyond the boardroom. They are the architects of narratives that inspire employees, reassure stakeholders and reinforce the organization's purpose.

In the C-Suite, where decisions are made at the speed of relevance, the CEO often becomes the embodiment of the company's values, vision and resilience. This visibility is a double-edged sword

– while it amplifies opportunities to connect and inspire, it also places immense pressure to navigate crises and manage scrutiny. Here, the Communications Officer's role becomes pivotal. They not only help craft the words but also shape the delivery, ensuring that every message aligns with the organization's core values and long-term goals.

But why does this partnership matter now more than ever? Because we are operating in an era defined by disruption. Technology has given everyone a voice, but it has also made the truth more vulnerable to distortion. Leaders must address societal expectations – from sustainability and diversity to ethics and governance – while meeting business objectives.

Navigating this complexity requires not only operational excellence but also a narrative that resonates across diverse audiences.

Charlotte Otter's book delves into the strategies, mindsets and tools necessary to elevate the CEO/Communications Officer partnership to a strategic advantage. It emphasizes the need for a proactive approach to executive presence – one that builds resilience rather than merely reacting to challenges. It explores how to establish authenticity as a cornerstone of leadership, creating a ripple effect that fosters trust both inside and outside the organization.

I am particularly inspired by the book's focus on mastering trust. Trust, after all, is the bedrock of every successful relationship, whether it's between a brand and its customers, an organization and its employees, or a CEO and their Communications Officer. Building trust requires alignment on values, a shared commitment to the truth, and the courage to confront challenges with integrity. These principles resonate deeply with me, not only as a leader but also as someone passionate about fostering cultures of respect and empowerment.

To every leader, communicator and changemaker reading this Foreword, I encourage you to embrace the lessons within these pages with an open mind and a resolute commitment to action. The world needs leaders who inspire trust, champion authenticity and steer their organizations with both vision and responsibility. As you turn these pages, may you find the inspiration and strategies to do just that.

Sindhu Gangadharan
Managing Director, SAP Labs India
Chairperson, NASSCOM; Board Member, Siemens India & Titan Company

Notes for the reader

The interviewees in *We Need New Leaders* are all real people. Some were happy for me to use their full names and that of their company, others preferred me to use their first name only, others chose a pseudonym. The quotes are all their own words, very lightly edited by me to remove repetition and filler words.

I asked all the interviewees to self-identify, so if I say someone is an immigrant, or a refugee, or queer, or Black, or a solo mama, this is because they have told me they identify this way.

There are several terms to describe the role of the head of communications. In my initial research sample alone, the titles of respondents vary from Senior Vice President of Strategy, Alliances and Communications to Senior Director Brand and Corporate Communications, to Chief Brand and Corporate Affairs Officer (and several others). For the purposes of simplicity, I refer to this role as Chief Communications Officer (CCO) and sometimes 'head of communication.' The 'chief' in CCO presumes that this is an executive committee or leadership team role. This is only sometimes the case, and where it is pertinent, I make this clear.

On the language of diversity, there are several terms in use to describe people who are not of the dominant, hegemonic work culture. The US favours underrepresented minorities (URM) as a general term that includes race, gender, physical disabilities, LGBTQIA+, class and language differences. I attempt to use this wherever possible, but also use 'leaders from diverse backgrounds.'

I also choose to lean on the idea of reputation rather than personal brand. This book will explain why.

Introduction

We've all had a bad boss, the 'my way or the highway' kind of person. Mostly, we sigh, blame ourselves a bit, chalk it up to experience and move on. Several factors indicate that the old school style of leadership is failing us on an epic scale. There's a burnout epidemic.[1] Employees report low engagement. CEOs and employees are at loggerheads on return to office policies. There are armies of coaches and phalanxes of leadership books both aiming to help leaders improve. There is another way: fostering great new leaders to take the helm and lead our organizations better. Some are there already, but in achingly small figures. This book hopes to help to swell their number.

I recently finished a Master of Science in Change Leadership. It was an excellent course, run jointly by HEC Paris and Oxford Saïd Business School over 18 months, with a cohort from all over the world. Having spent most of my career working with executives on reputation, I wrote my master's thesis on how the CEO and the head of communications build trust to manage and mitigate reputational risk.

The course has existed in various forms for 20 years, and has a dedicated alumni group that meets twice a year. We did hundreds of readings on change – how to effect change as an individual, for a team, for a company and for complex global change. The goal of the course was to equip us with the tools to become change leaders.

Having learned how to be a change leader, I wanted to explore how we change leaders.

This book is for new and aspiring leaders, especially those from diverse backgrounds. It acts as a companion as they start their leadership journey, whether it's from the moment they acknowledge to themselves that they want to become leaders or when they sign the contract to take on the role. It's also for the communicators in their team, for whom CEO and senior leadership reputation is a halo for company reputation. And it's also for founders, for whom creating a convincing founder narrative is critical for finding investment.

In it you will learn why reputation matters not just for the company but also for the CEO, how the CEO and the head of communications build trust to manage reputational risk, and the building blocks of reputation from over 60 interviews with leaders and communicators from all over the world.

Why do we need new leaders?

We Need New Leaders was born out of my conviction that the current style of leadership – top-down, autocratic, paternalistic, mechanistic, transactional – is failing us. The new leaders who emerge are having to battle the same system that employees are in. How are they managing? What are the skills do they have that have enabled them to rise above the fray and to leadership positions? And who can they partner with in the organization to ensure that their record of success is visible to all?

In addition, the book emerged from my own leadership and reputation building experience. I ran a global team of executive and employee communicators for a number of years. As an executive with a diverse background (female in a tech company, creative amongst scientists, South African in Germany, introvert, going through perimenopause), I consistently achieved high leadership trust scores and empowered those around me. I was building my own reputation, while doing the same for board members and other senior leaders – and simultaneously managing large internal change programmes and the reputational crises that arose.

To understand better how other leaders from diverse backgrounds managed their own leadership journeys, I interviewed over 40 people with heterogenous identities and backgrounds. I wanted to talk to people who don't look or identify like 90% of the leaders in the US, the UK and Europe.

I interviewed people who are data scientists, large carnivore researchers, software company presidents, fashion designers, founders, heads of PR agencies, people who have been CEOs of several companies, current CEOs, heads of HR, board members, shipping brokers, politicians, consultants, leaders of global sales teams and people in philanthropy. In addition to holding senior roles, the interviewees held one or more identities: female, person of colour, neurodiverse, LGBTQIA+, of working-class, refugee or migrant background, in a caring role, primary parent, introvert, menopausal and with physical disabilities. I also spoke to leaders who work remotely, without the in-presence magnet of the office to draw their employees to one place.

They showed several commonalities in how they lead that I reflect throughout the book. I was especially interested to learn how their leadership, their identity and their reputation intersect.

However, these leaders, wonderful as they are, are all meeting barriers in the workplace. Diversity and inclusion teams have suddenly become political and expendable. Women, while gaining board positions, are not gaining CEO roles at the same rate. The number of people of colour in CEO positions in Europe, the US and the UK is laughable. And that's not to mention people with physical disabilities and neurodiversities; people who are trans, non-binary and LGBTQIA+; people who wish lead to fractionally, part-time or remotely; people with caring responsibilities, both for children and elders; people going through unseen hormonal change or suffering from auto-immune illnesses; people from working-class or migrant and refugee backgrounds. They all face hurdles.

I began to wonder, like Carrie Bradshaw, could the skills of reputation management help emerging leaders land, keep and create their dream leadership roles, and so increase the number of new leaders in the workplace and reduce their hurdles?

Is reputation key to helping diverse leaders succeed?

This book is the answer to those questions.

How the book is organized

The first part of the book focuses on new leadership priorities. We are in a leadership crisis – both *of* leaders (the transactional, paternalistic style I describe above) and *for* leaders, who have to navigate a complex, multi-crisis world.

Part of the crisis of leaders is our reliance on an old model. Professor of business psychology at London Business School, Tomas Chamarro-Premuzic, puts it more starkly than me: 'There is a pathological mismatch between the attributes that seduce us in a leader and those that are needed to become an effective leader.'[2] He says we are unable to detect incompetence in men because we have a flawed leadership archetype that mistakes confidence for competence.

The crisis of leaders is personal, but the crisis for leaders is contextual. Like all of us, they operate in a world where geopolitics can't be ignored. Climate, war, AI, cyber-security, misinformation, elections, regulatory changes and the fallout from a global pandemic all continue to affect business and decision-makers, as well as ordinary citizens. With the loss of trust in media and politics so ably documented by Edelman in their annual survey,[3] leaders are now expected to take a stance on issues and lead the way for their employees, partners, allies, audiences and communities.

On top of this, growth – that business imperative that orients the seasonal swing of any publically listed company towards announcing results four times a year – is being questioned by those who believe the planet can't withstand more growth. Data, on which our cherished new artificial and apparently super-intelligent friend relies, consumes energy at an offensive rate.

The leadership context is extremely tough. And it's even harder for diverse leaders, as the role of diversity, equity and inclusion (DEI, the strategic mechanism by which most companies attract, hire, retain and reward diverse talent) is being called into question. In Chapter 2, I address some of the challenges that DEI is currently facing as a function, talk to a number of DEI thought leaders who are sparking change from the outside in, and reflect on an interview with a leader who runs the deaf advocacy employee resource group at a global company.

Using examples from the interviews, I show in Chapter 3 how emerging leaders landed or created their dream leadership roles, and some common factors in how they think about leadership. Early leaders are starting to build their reputation, not always consciously, by how they behave and how they think about communication.

Chapter 4 details how more senior leaders lead for longevity, their conditions for success and their personal leadership style. They demonstrate extremely high awareness of their leadership and communications approach and focus on listening as much as speaking. More senior leaders are consciously building their reputation by ensuring their words and actions match.

A common factor for both emerging and senior leaders is that they are incredibly thoughtful about how they use language and create meaning. Words matter. Combined with consistent action, words are the building blocks of a leader's reputation.

Being a leader from a diverse background can be lonely, and it's my contention that there's a potential workplace partnership that many leaders are ignoring or not making the most of. The second part of the book focuses on new relationship metrics with their reputation partner. With a very short introduction into some of the key reputation concepts, Chapter 5 shows that while we cannot absolutely control our reputation, understanding how it works helps us build one.

In Chapter 6, I show the differences and similarities between corporate reputation and CEO reputation. Leaders from diverse backgrounds looking to land and keep the top jobs can learn lessons from how CEOs build their reputation, especially around the idea of reputation portability.

Crisis is the reason most CEOs hire heads of communication – they want someone as their partner when things get ugly. In Chapter 7, I give some examples of CEOs who have handled crisis well and those who have not. I also talk about the glass cliff, which is a challenge diverse leaders face.

The leadership crisis is personal and contextual, and the only person in or near the C-Suite who can give the CEO advice on both is the chief communications officer. This is especially so for the diverse leader who faces exponential threats and challenges to their leadership – they may find unexpected support from the CCO whose goal it is to protect both the company and the CEO's reputations. The underlying dynamics of the relationship could protect a diverse leader's tenure from being too short. This is the focus of Chapter 8.

In the third part of this book, I explore the new reputation equity. In Chapter 9, I look at the good, the bad and the ugly of the CEO/CCO relationship, how trust can be built and how it can be broken.

In Chapter 10, I cover reputation management for diverse leaders who are not yet CEOs. Combining insights from the interviews from a range of leaders at different stages in their careers with my experience of working with executives, I highlight the process of reputation building and why this matters for leaders who do not look like or seem like the homogenous or default 'norm.'

Founders sit in a category of their own, and Chapter 11 focuses on the role of reputation building for founders. Diverse founders historically receive much less funding than non-diverse founders and have to face the cognitive bias of investors. This chapter shows how some of the rules of reputation management can help them break through.

In Chapter 12, the final chapter, I look at how we move towards a cohort of new leaders, building on the lessons we've learned in this book. While many of the problems we face are systemic, leaders from diverse backgrounds or of diverse identities can take heart. They are the leaders we need in this moment.

Conclusion

As I've researched and interviewed around this topic, I've come to realize that leadership is not an artefact. It's not an object passed from one leader to another in a meritocratic relay race. Instead, it's a living thing that must be tended and nurtured. Bad leadership infects and toxifies its environment, but good leadership provides nutrients for others to grow.

One of the functions of leadership is to create meaning – for employees so that they understand the strategic goals of the business and their role in that. But leaders are also there to create meaning for all audiences – customers, partners, suppliers, investors, the media, general public and their peers in the C-Suite.

Meaning starts with the messenger. Leaders need to understand themselves and be clear on what they stand for. The next step is to communicate that meaning and how they do that, and what they say, is reputational. Reputation is always two way. We cannot control it. However, the more our words and our behaviour match, the more authentically and intentionally we show up, the more trust we build. Trust – built on a consistent reputation based on what individual leaders say and how they behave combined with what others say about them – is critical for leaders from diverse identities and backgrounds to land and keep the top jobs.

As the reputation managers of a business, the communications team or the chief communications officer (CCO) is the best person to help leaders build that reputation in a trusting, meaningful way.

A note about the title

My home country, South Africa, recently had its sixth election as a democracy. The ANC, which has governed for 30 years, did not win a majority and had to build a government of national unity with other political parties. We live in a world when a peaceful transition from one government to another is not a given, and I was amongst those who watched proudly as they achieved this. One of the smaller parties, Rise Mzansi, whose leader Songezo Zibi was elected to the National Assembly, had as its tagline 'We Need New Leaders'. This was my inspiration as I started to think about how reputation, leadership and diversity might converge.

Part 1

New leadership priorities

Many of the leaders we have are not the leaders we need in this moment. The movement towards growing diversity, equity and inclusion has been hijacked by culture war politics, impeding the hiring and promotion of leaders from diverse backgrounds across all leadership levels in organizations. Increasing societal diversity needs to be represented in companies. This is an innovation priority as well as a question of social justice. While systemic change is slow, and hurdles are evident, leaders from diverse backgrounds are finding, keeping and creating their dream jobs. In this part, we hear from them and see what we can learn from their experience towards a new kind of leadership.

Chapter 1

The leadership crisis

Through almost any lens, our current context is not great. We live in a world at war. The planet is discernably hotter. A very small number of people are growing richer and richer, a very large number of people are staying very poor and the middle classes are embattled. Despite more awareness, we're failing to stem sexual violence and violence against those who are demonstrably other. Every election makes us hold our collective breath because it could change everything.

Because it's slow, it feels organic. But it is not. Every one of these things follows a leadership decision. Leaders decide to bomb civilians. Leaders decide not to fine or contain fossil fuel companies. Leaders decide not to tax billionaires. Leaders decide not to prosecute people who commit sexual violence or to educate soldiers that rape and torture are not legitimate tools of war.

You may say we live in a terrible world. I say we live in a world run by terrible leaders with reputations for terrible behaviour.

Amongst them are many good leaders. The terrible conditions, while not of their own choosing, impact how they lead. They have to navigate the context, act competently, make decisions, explain why they are making them and stand for something so that their employees and citizens in the communities in which they operate understand who they are and whether to follow them or not. Their ability to do so, either well or poorly, is reputational.

The leadership crisis we are in is both a crisis *of* leaders (behaviour and personal traits that create our context, and which we reward) and a crisis *for* leaders (a context that challenges them personally).

The crisis of leaders

There is a big gap between the proto-dictators of our time, and leaders of business. However, there is a spectrum of leadership behaviour that we recognize as the norm. Through centuries of experience that has accreted in our brains, we have come to believe that leadership looks, sounds and feels a certain way.

To us, leadership might be loud. It might be big. It might have a room-owning energy. It might seem always confident. It might be back-slappingly supported by others of its type. It might fail upwards. It might take advantage of those who are weaker in social capital. It might mock or exclude those who are other to it. It might engage in exclusive social activities. It might claim other people's success as its own. It might hire, reward, promote and retain only those who resemble it.

Leaders like this have got us to where we are today.

This is because we have a flawed leadership archetype that mistakes confidence for competence. Tomas Chamorro-Premuzic, whose 2013 *Harvard Business Review* article 'Why Do So Many Incompetent Men Become Leaders?' is one of the most-read articles on that site, encapsulates this in his eponymous book. His take is that it's not the perceived glass ceiling for women that's the problem so much as 'the lack of career obstacles for incompetent men.'[1] In the book, Chamorro-Premuzic explores the relationship between leadership and the toxic traits of narcissism and psychopathy. He quotes various studies that estimate the rate of psychopathy in senior management roles at between 4–20%; and the rate of narcissism (1% in the general population) amongst CEOs at 5%. 'Both traits are also more likely to be found in men than in women. For instance, the rate of clinical narcissism is almost 40% higher in men than in women… Meanwhile, psychopathy occurs three times more often in men than it does in women.'[2]

These traits, he says, help people advance their careers but hurt the people and the organizations they lead. We are so entranced by the confidence and charisma these people exude that we do not recognize that they are not good leaders.

Kholi, who is the Southern African MD of a global multinational, spoke to this conflation in our interview:

> 'Sometimes our brains have been wired to think that people who look intelligent and come across as charming are intelligent, whereas we might be missing the most intelligent who would actually provide a significant input. What I've learned over the years is how I can spot within my team the person who will actually help me take my organization forward rather than the loudest and the smartest. And I think in a sales context, there are so many of those, and one mistake you will make is focusing only on the loudest. You must be able to have that capability to sift through that to find the expertise you need.'

Our systems of understanding lead us to think we know what a leader looks, sounds and behaves like. These systems make it harder for us to break the mould, and so the hurdles for women, men who do not look like the norm, people of colour and those who present as non-binary are set even higher. Mary Ann Sieghart's book *The Authority Gap* defines bias as the flip side of privilege,[3] and it's our systems of understanding that bias us against leaders who don't look like the dominant norm.

Let's take a brief look at these.

The systems we are up against

While this book looks at leadership from an individual lens, it's important to state from the outset that many of the problems are systemic. I've teased out some of the systemic strands but they are all woven together into a thick rope of separation that threads through society. And while many organizations or businesses lay claim to a modern sensibility that would never actively reflect them, the systemic problems are pervasive – in the society in which employees are raised, in the images of the organization or the metaphors it uses to describe itself and how these play out for individuals trying to succeed at work. It may seem systemic, but it is experienced as personal.

Gareth Morgan's book *Images of Organization* is a management literature classic. In it, he references several metaphors that organizations employ whether wittingly or not. Morgan says 'the evidence for a patriarchal view of organization is easy to see.'[4] Men were socialized to take management roles; women were socialized to take more subordinate roles. As women started to take on more leadership roles, Morgan says, they were still socialized to appear as rational and analytic (like men) and to downplay any qualities the patriarchy sees as female, such as intuition, nurturing and empathy. 'So long as organizations are dominated by patriarchal values, the roles of women in organizations will always be played out on "male" terms.'[5]

At their best, these values are paternalistic; at their worst, authoritarian. To create change for leaders and employees alike, we need to learn to value different human qualities.

Another archetype that besets us at work, and which the masculine archetype plays into because of its top-down command-and-control nature, is the mechanistic one. We're all cogs in the machine, each being maximized for profit. This is a metaphor that grew out of the Industrial Revolution. In the twentieth century, it morphed into organizational systems that bureaucratized human output (think of Henry Ford's production line, clocking in and out, spans of control, goals, objectives and rationalization) and this has not yet left us.

As Gareth Morgan says, 'One of the most basic problems of modern management is that the mechanical way of thinking is so ingrained in our everyday conceptions of organization that it is often very difficult to organize in any other way.'[6]

This system of understanding leads us to think that good leaders are good controllers, and employees are silent and obedient. There is little space for change, unless decreed from above, little flexibility, people become passive and the atmosphere is fear-based. However, we do see resistance to this as employees are now more choosy about where they work and adjudicate future employers based on company policy and purpose. The battle currently being played out, which researchers call the 'Great Disconnect', is a symbol of employees' resistance to being told to return to the office, despite having been incredibly productive during the pandemic.[7] The leaders who insist on returns to office risk being seen as controlling, old-fashioned and autocratic.

The quarterly pursuit of results above building long-term value is another system of understanding that affects how we experience leaders. Renowned British economist Sir John Kay's recent book *The Corporation in the 21st Century* describes how the pursuit of shareholder value has destroyed some of the leading companies of the twentieth century. In it, he talks about the tensions between 'stakeholder capitalism or shareholder priority' and calls those who presume the two are aligned 'naïve.'[8] In our current understanding, good leaders lay off employees in order to deliver quarterly shareholder value, or, as in the case of Boeing, systematically underprivilege innovation and market leadership for shareholder value allowing its competitor Airbus' A320 to overtake the 737 as the bestselling aircraft in history.[9]

These paternalistic, bureaucratic and short-term systems embrace a transactional form of leadership in which employees are rewarded for doing what they are told and punished for not. The stick-and-carrot leadership style that this engenders is not working, and is partially responsible for the burnout epidemic.[10]

A recent meta-analysis on workplace aggression (471 studies, across 36 countries and totalling nearly 150,000 people) showed that it is harmful to performance.[11] Kim Scott, who was an executive at Google and Apple before going on to write her acclaimed book *Radical Candor*, says that:

> 'command and control can hinder innovation and harm a team's ability to improve the efficiency of routine work. Bosses and companies get better results when they voluntarily lay down unilateral power and encourage their teams and peers to hold them accountable, when they quit trying to control employees and focus instead on encouraging agency.'[12]

An alternative is transformational leadership, in which leaders seek to inspire, motivate and engage.[13] However, the challenge with transformational leadership is when a leader's behaviour doesn't match their inspiring promises – it appears to have a dark side.[14] An example of this is Elizabeth Holmes of Theranos, who inspired employees and investors alike with her vision of cheaper, more accessible blood tests that later turned out to be fraudulent.

The leadership crisis is a crisis of leaders, in that we have the wrong people in place, creating the context in which we all live, shoring up rather than breaking down systemic problems. The fear-based, masculinist leadership style contributes to a context. That context – war, climate breakdown, political instability, violence against women and minorities, job instability, the rise of a billionaire class – creates a crisis for leaders.

The crisis for leaders

We live in a complex, multi-crisis world and no business exists context-free. Other geopolitical pressures include the rise of AI, the increased regulatory environment, mis- and disinformation, and the ongoing friction between employees and leaders on return to work policies.

Edelman's 2022 Trust Barometer found that nearly one out of two of their 36,000 survey respondents view government and media as divisive forces, and people want more leadership from business.[15] Their 2023 report showed again that business is the most trusted institution and is expected to 'inform debate and deliver solutions on climate, DEI and skill training.'[16] And in 2024, while the media is still actively mistrusted, and trust in business is falling, business is still expected to deliver the most innovation to society.[17]

The pattern is there: in a world where trust is being eroded, people look to business as the most trusted institution and the place from where societal innovation must be delivered.

So on top of all the pressures of leading a business, inspiring employees, assuring all the various audiences, growing and innovating, business leaders also need to stand up for society. Leaders need to have a deep understanding of a number of topics external to their business and take a meaningful position on them. This is why I say this is a crisis for leaders: they carry a weight on their shoulders.

Rise of social media

Just as the paternalistic, mechanistic and transactional styles of leadership were beginning to be replaced by transformational leadership, social media arrived to hold up a mirror to everything a leader says and does. When I was leading executive communications, we received constant requests from employees, the DEI and social media team for executive commentary on breaking news. And in the moment, we had to adjudicate the request, get the executive's buy-in and huddle with them on the nuances of the response.

And it's a tightrope walk, because, with social media, everything a leader says is flashed around the world in an instant and remains on the public record for eternity. It's reputational. Social media – and the blurring of boundaries between internal and external communication – has completely changed the leadership game.

But a leader can't respond to every breaking news event. If they speak on everything that happens in the world, they become a broadcast outlet and neglect their role in business. What they comment on becomes just as important on how they comment. It's important for leaders to find a pathway through the social media jungle that is authentic to them, meaningful for their audiences, represents their business fairly, and shows their employees and external partners and audiences not only how much they care but that they care about the right things.

An additional challenge with social media is the amount of digital noise. Leaders need to have a strong point of view, backed up with insights and opinions, to break through for the right reasons.

Putting reputation at risk

What you say in response to a major world event is one thing; how you act is another. Acting too slowly, or not acting at all, can also be reputational.

When Russia invaded Ukraine on 24 February, 2022, the world was shocked. Many leaders adopted a wait-and-see attitude, perhaps hoping the war would be over quickly. Martin Böhringer and the leadership team of Staffbase, a German scale-up that creates software for communications professionals, acted at lightning speed. One of their customers was a Russian state-owned business that Martin believed was using his company's products to justify the war. This was against Staffbase's people-centred values. He cancelled the contract on 24 February – having never done anything like this before – and posted the entire letter with the company's name redacted on his personal LinkedIn.[18]

Compare this to other companies that dragged their feet about exiting Russia, and as a result damaged their reputations. Jeffrey Sonnenfeld and his team at the Yale Chief Executive Leadership Institute began keeping an active list shortly after the war started. Only when the list was made public, did companies like Starbucks, Coca-Cola and McDonald's pull out.[19]

How, and how fast, companies act in response to major world events signals their values to the world. And any gap between what they say (their values) and what they do is a risk to reputation and threatens to break trust between the company and its audiences.

When companies start to try to explain the gap, this is what we call 'spin.' Rupert Younger, who runs the Oxford University Centre for Corporate Reputation, says that 'spin occurs when the story told begins to diverge too far from the reality.' [20]

A recent example of this is the Kyte Baby scandal that broke in January 2024. Kyte Baby is an alternative baby clothes company that espouses strong parent-friendly values. However, when an employee requested the right to remote work when she and her partner adopted a baby who was born at 22 weeks and needed intensive care, she was fired.

After her sister made a TikTok video explaining what had happened, the Kyte Baby CEO responded with her own video saying she apologized to the employee for how her parental leave was handled and that the company would examine their leave policies. She came under fire for this – criticisms included that it seemed insincere, scripted and not enough. The CEO returned the next day with an unscripted video apologizing more, saying she regretted her 'terrible decision' not to let the employee work remotely.

The story made media headlines, including on CNN.[21] No CEO wants to make CNN for the wrong reasons. She compounded her error (firing) by trying to spin the story (first apology) and then hit the headlines for the wrong reasons (second apology).

The gap is dangerous territory and is best handled by being as transparent as possible, as sincere and humane as possible, as quickly as possible. Or don't behave badly in the first place.

CEOs behaving badly is a different reputational game from CEOs communicating bad news. Bad news is not uncommon in corporate life, but it's how leaders handle it that differs. This was made starkly obvious with the layoffs in the tech industry between 2022 and 2024, and how different CEOs handled the messaging. (I cover this in more detail in Chapter 7.)

Conclusion

We are in a leadership crisis that is both of and for leaders. Bad leadership behaviour creates the context in which we live; good leaders have to find a pathway to success in that context. Whether they are good or bad, transactional or transformative, people look to business leaders for innovation and solutions because they no longer trust governments or the press.

The way we think about work today is beset by systems of understanding that are centuries-old, and so implicit now that even mentioning one of them in a work context is likely to elicit surprise, if not rage. However, they are still there, threaded through our private and work lives, and informing our decisions and how companies attract, hire, retain and reward people who are not of the dominant work culture.

As we will see, companies and leaders gain reputations for character and competence. However, leaders are now expected to provide coherence for all audiences who feel confused and worried in the current context. You will see these aspects of reputation threaded throughout the chapters that follow. They are important for leaders seeking to build great reputations, and for communicators seeking to create a solid relationship with a CEO or leader.

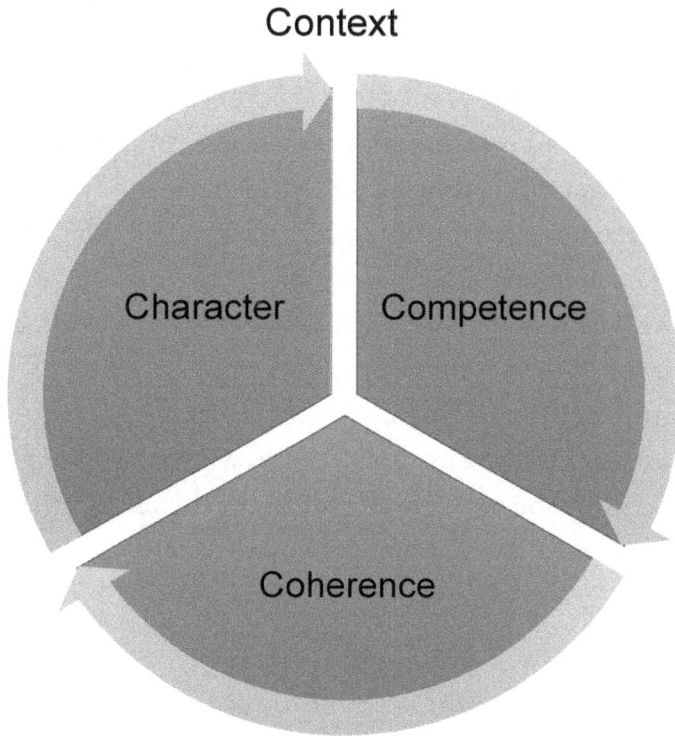

Context

Character Competence

Coherence

Figure 1: Aspects of reputation

Leaders who are conscientious about both company and their own reputation will build good relationships with their communicators. Leaders from diverse backgrounds or underrepresented minorities can partner with a communicator to foster career longevity and their next great leadership role. Under the overarching banner of protecting reputation, CCOs and the communications team will help leaders demonstrate character and competence, while creating coherence in confusing, contested and complex times.

From this chapter: Lessons in leadership communication

- Trust in politics and the media has dwindled to such an extent that people look to business as the most trusted institution.
- Social media has eroded the corporate boundaries between internal and external so that bad leadership behaviour is no longer protected by a wall of silence.
- Trust is lost when companies try to explain the gap between their values and their behaviour.
- The bedrock of our workplace culture is still paternalistic, autocratic and short-termist and employees are miserable, burnt-out and failing to relate to leaders.
- However, transformational leaders who focus on engaging, inspiring and exciting employees are better positioned to lead in an uncertain future.

Chapter 2

Diversity still matters

It's estimated that since the murder of George Floyd in May 2020, companies around the world have pledged $340 billion to racial equity.[1] According to Shelley Stewart who leads the McKinsey Institute for Black Economic Mobility, the money was committed to activities in and outside companies to both 'raise the floor and lift the ceiling.'

Despite the pledges, there's a growing backlash against overt diversity, inclusion and equity (DEI) programmes. Since the layoffs at technology companies began in 2022, these companies have retrenched, downsized or redeployed their DEI teams: Amazon, Microsoft, Google, Meta, Zoom, Snap, Tesla, DoorDash, Lyft, Red Hat, Home Depot, Wayfair and John Deere, amongst others.[2]

At the same time as DEI teams being slashed, we're still nowhere near achieving equity in leadership.

The facts

At the time of writing, only 10.4% of US Fortune 500 companies have female CEOs and this number has not moved since 2023. And it's worse for Black female CEOs. After Walgreens replaced Roz Brewer with a male CEO, this left only TIAA CEO Thasunda Brown Duckett and SAIC CEO Toni Townes-Whitley, whom Fortune magazine says, 'took over in a rare female CEO-to-female CEO handoff.'[3] Fortune 500 companies have eight Black CEOs in total.[4]

And the same goes for the UK. The FTSE Women Leaders Review, which came out in February 2024, showed that while the proportion of women on boards in FTSE 100 companies rose to 42% in 2024, there are only ten female CEOs. In the FTSE 350, there are 21 female CEOs.[5]

In Fortune's debut list of female CEOs of the top 500 European companies in 2024 (based on revenue), there are seven women who are CEOs.[6] One of these is Margherita Della Valle, CEO of Vodafone, who also appears on the FTSE 100 list. So, if we're counting, and I definitely am, there are 16 female CEOs in the top 600 companies across the EU and the UK. None are Black or of ethnic minority background.

The Parker Review has been tracking ethnicity in leadership in the UK since 2015. While 96% of listed companies in their latest survey stated that they have met the target of having at least one ethnic minority director on their board, there are still only 12 ethnic minority CEOs in the FTSE 100 (an increase of six from 2022), and 14 in the FTSE 250.[7]

Both the FTSE Women Leaders Review and the Parker Review report improvement in representation overall, but people from diverse backgrounds are still not getting the top jobs. Progress is both glacial, and as the Parker Review says, 'anaemic.'

The current situation is that companies are slashing DEI programmes, and progress in getting adequate representation at the highest levels of companies is slow.

Apart from waiting for Boards and senior hiring committees to change how they hire at the current glacial and anaemic pace, what can be done?

The changing face of DEI

According to Porter Braswell, corporate DEI will only survive if it moves out of its current siloes and is integrated across all departments and all levels of the organization. Porter is the CEO and founder of 2045 Studio (which references the year that the US will be majority racially diverse) and the founder of an inclusive generative AI platform JodieAI. 2045 Studio helps companies transform their work culture into an inclusive environment where all employees feel empowered to succeed. After Yale, Porter worked at Goldman Sachs for three years until – to the horror of his parents – decided to leave to start his first company, recruitment platform called Jopwell that helps Black, Latinx and Indigenous American professionals seek career advancement. Porter sold the business after eight years to True Search, a global executive recruitment platform, and recently became MD at True.

He is the author of a book called *Let Them See You*, is on the boards of several companies, is a regular contributor to thought leadership articles on *Fast Company* and other publications, and the host of Race at Work, a *Harvard Business Review* podcast. Porter identifies as a Black man. He is married, and when we spoke, was awaiting the birth of his third child. In a recent *Fast Company* article, Porter says corporate DEI programmes as we know them will not survive beyond 2025.[8]

I interviewed him from his office in New York, and he told me:

'If a company has invested in DEI programmes or strategies over the last decade, which are most publicly traded companies, they are now facing what I'm coining the Inclusion Gap. And the Inclusion Gap, in my opinion, means that companies are going to have to move from a siloed experience (Chief Diversity Officer, diversity division, diversity programme) into a distributed experience, where all individuals within a company are tasked locally with building the principles of DEI and inclusive cultures on their team level. And for that gap to be closed, companies have to invest in technology, external communities, learning and development, to really transition people managers to now be on the front lines of these principles and to own those principles of DEI.'

All three of Porter's businesses since leaving banking have been fuelled by creating inclusivity, and 2045 Studio supports companies in building the cultures in which all can thrive.

Porter acknowledges that this is hard to do but says that everyone in a company needs to feel included in the DEI dialogue and narrative. 'The role that they play will be different based on their realities and their existence of what it means to operate within that company. So, every company has to kind of take this general framework but make it customized for their unique needs where they find themselves along this journey.'[9] For Porter, managers need to become inclusive leaders. (I will cover this in more detail in Chapter 12.)

DEI is multilayered

Angie Vaux agrees with Porter that DEI is not a simple fix. Angie grew up in Birmingham in the UK and describes a childhood in which her parents struggled financially. She was the first person in her family to go to university, and on graduating, received seven job offers. She got her first managerial role in a large tech company in her twenties, skipped several levels and was soon running a huge regional team with profit and loss responsibilities.

Angie is now the CEO of Women in Tech forum, a business that she started after leaving corporate. It is a forum with 15,000 members worldwide. Women in Tech forum has a two-part business model: on the one hand, they work with companies to improve their employer branding and help them attract more female talent into the organization. On the other, they focus on talent retention by offering an annual subscription to their professional development programme that is specifically for women's employee resource groups (ERGs). There is also a career development platform filled with resources.

Angie identifies as a female leader, from a working-class background, and someone who has been both a single mother and sole breadwinner (though she has recently remarried). She describes some of the challenges she faced as a woman in tech: 'When I started my career, I was often the only woman in the room in a very white, very middle-aged, male-dominated environment. The boys' club was still very much alive.'

Angie stops in her story to say she believes the boys' club is still alive in some organizations and based on outdated organizational structures created by men for men. Then she continues the anecdote:

'I remember sitting at the back of a plane, all the way to New Orleans with a couple of my marketing colleagues. All the sales team were in business class at the front. My colleague, who was my peer, asked me how much I earned. My area was doing very well. Overachieving. The P&L was significantly bigger than his. Anyway, it was an odd question to ask, particularly back then, but it transpired that he earned triple what I earned while running a much smaller organization.

I went and asked my boss's boss at the time for a pay increase. Since he knew my partner, who was very successful in tech, he said, "you don't need any extra money, Angie." And when I split up with my partner, my salary didn't even cover my mortgage. I just went and informed them that I would be looking for another job because I didn't want to lose my house.'

Angie says when she told her management that she was leaving, her salary doubled overnight, and within nine months, went up again. 'This doesn't typically happen to a man. It's a generalization, but men are much more assertive when it comes to their salary negotiations. They just have to create the illusion that they can do the work. And women typically have to prove themselves first.'

For Angie, the challenge with DEI is multilayered:

'It isn't just a simple fix. It's not just the domain of HR or the DEI manager, it is actually the responsibility of everybody within the organization, from the CEO, the board, to individual contributors, to managers at every level. It does require a concerted effort from every single person in the organization to really drive that change and to drive these inclusive work practices.'

Angie and Porter agree that DEI – or real change – takes every-body within the organization and a willingness to create change. For Porter, managers are key. And inclusive managers aren't only thinking about including people of colour and women; they need to be inclusive of all identities.

Case study: Navigating work with a perceived disability

Lee is the employee advocate for the deaf and hard-of-hearing community at a large Europe-based technology company. When I interviewed him, he was feeling frustrated and emotional. He had requested subtitles at an in-person session at work and had been refused.

'It leaves me speechless. We have the technology. I'm using it now. It's free. It's built in and it works.' (I was interviewing Lee on MS Teams which accommodates instant subtitling.) 'And then I tell the organizer who just refuses it, you know? So, then I have the work of escalating it, which isn't a pleasant thing to have to do. And you know, I'm having to inform people for my network, which has to be anonymous because of deaf colleagues who are not disclosed.'

Since Lee's hearing loss began in 2007, he has been an advocate for the deaf and hard-of-hearing community of employees at the company and is now the global co-lead of a network of employee volunteers. He says being hard of hearing is seldom visible (unless someone is wearing a hearing aid openly), and while there are 50 members with hearing loss in the community, there are probably many more who either haven't yet acknowledged their hearing loss, or don't want to, out of fear of stigma. Lee also believes that his 'out' position as an employee advocate helps in some ways but also means he is sometimes not considered for specific tasks or jobs which he would be capable of doing well.

On top of his full-time job at the company, Lee feels the burden of continually having to advocate for the community. He describes his advocacy as a fight. His manager is compassionate and supports him in these extra tasks, but they do eat into his working hours and private life. It also takes a lot of extra energy, especially if people are not receptive to feedback and he is then forced to escalate to get the problem solved. When people are receptive, Lee then educates them on the steps they need to take to provide accessibility. He often consults to IT or other employee networks on how they can make accessibility improvements.

And in the light of the layoffs in tech, Lee also says that employees who are hard of hearing try to remain incognito. 'The cards aren't stacked in our favour when it comes to career progression. And when somebody's been fired, we know that it's multiple times more difficult for them to get a job than somebody with full hearing.'

The biggest challenge that hard-of-hearing or other people with perceived disabilities face is the return to office mandates. During the pandemic, when everyone worked from home, all employees with disabilities were able to set up their technology and workspaces in the way that suited them. Now, post-Covid, hybrid working is increasingly difficult for those with a disability.

'The trend is now back to pre-pandemic times. They're trying to force us to be on site basically. And what leaders probably don't realize is this excludes people. If you're in a wheelchair, you're going to have to make a trip for a 30-minute info session. That's not always practical. If you're blind, you're potentially going to need somebody to accompany you to help you make your way there as well. If you're deaf, you're going to need subtitles at the venue as you would when you are at your desk. I'm not saying we'd all prefer to be at home, but when we are on site, an accessible set-up needs to be in place without having to request it every time.'

With the European Accessibility Act coming into force in 2025, companies now have to ensure that all meetings and employee and customer interactions, whether online or in person, are completely accessible. But until then, Lee's fight goes on. And, he says wryly, probably after the Act comes into place as well.

Think about Lee's position. He has a full-time job with tough goals to achieve and advocates constantly for his community – with leaders, managers and other employees. He is carrying an additional load that eats into his private time, preys on his mind and emotions and potentially gets in the way of promotion or new opportunities. Exclusionary behaviours – such as forgetting or neglecting to provide subtitles at an in-person meeting – exact a toll on employees that many of the interviewees describe as a weight or a burden.

Companies are starting to acknowledge how that weight affects employees and interrogate how they might lighten the load. An example of this is the emerging focus on the effects of menopause on women in the workplace. Five years ago, this was just not happening. I remember calling my boss in floods of tears from Beijing when an executive keynote had not gone 100% to plan. I had never cried openly at work before, and I had no idea I was going through hormonal hell. That moment broke something in my relationship with my manager and we were never on an even footing again. Imagine if I'd had the wherewithal to explain what was happening to me physically and emotionally, and if she'd had the awareness training to help me get the support I needed, then perhaps our relationship would have remained in better balance.

Activating inclusivity

In planning this book, I made sure I interviewed a range of leaders from different backgrounds, and what I found is that many acknowledge more than one identity. Two of the leaders whom I interviewed work in the education and training space, empowering employees to self-advocate and helping businesses become more inclusive – while talking in an open way about how they identify. By talking about their identities and personal challenges in a work environment, they open space for others to do the same.

Breaking taboos

Jess Rad identifies as a social entrepreneur, a women's advocate, a neurodivergent woman, a parent carer, someone who has been through premature menopause and who is half-Persian. She is an ADHD-er with autistic traits and calls herself a solo mama (which she explains to me is her way of reframing as positive the negative shadow around the term 'single mother.')

Jess is founder and director of The Womenhood, which is a platform based in the UK devoted to advancing gender equity by addressing the unspoken challenges of womanhood. The business began with an event series called 'The Unspoken Sessions' for talented women to share their stories, wisdom and expertise with others to create space for knowledge sharing, learning, and peer-to-peer support and now supports organizations to close their gender gaps. Her goal is to unite all genders through the creation of safe and brave spaces, to improve compassion and empathy for the hidden challenges impacting women today.

Jess says that now she is called on to deliver inclusivity programmes for companies on topics that include women's health, neurodiversity, money and relationships, and menopause. She says: 'And now I'm starting to talk about being a parent carer as well, because the additional needs of children require additional needs of parents, including our time, energy and money. These are disproportionately impacting women as we are often the primary caregivers.'

Jess, who recently won an award for being a Positive Role Model for Gender in the UK from 90,000 other nominations, believes her role is to break taboos. 'I'm doing my very best to speak very openly and honestly, to destigmatize things that are often hidden behind closed doors. I like the idea of being a voice for people that don't feel able to do that.'

Gillian Jones-Williams is a multi-award-winning managing director of a leadership development consultancy in the UK that she founded over 30 years ago and the author of several books on coaching. Shortly after our interview, she was awarded Businesswoman of the Decade in the UK's Best Businesswomen's Awards 2024. The consultancy has eight employees and 40 associates. She identifies as a female leader, from a working-class background, a working parent who has been through menopause and who is neurodiverse. She has cyclothymia (a less extreme form of bipolar disorder (BD)), ADHD and rejection sensitivity dysphoria (RSD).

Her business focuses largely on helping companies with diversity and inclusion, including programmes to support those from diverse backgrounds. She now discloses her neurodiversity to clients, and she finds that people are grateful for her openness. Gillian believes that companies are open to candidates with ADHD, but that they haven't yet worked out what the benefits of bipolar are (she says people with BD are 'very, very creative'). She says there are probably lots of people who have BD who are on medication, high functioning and in jobs, but they are less likely to disclose their status during a job interview.

Gillian, who started work at 16, is most proud of her award-winning women's development programme, Rise, which she developed seven years ago. She now runs it internationally and has trained nearly 3,000 women. She says: 'Just seeing women go through this and changing their lives, helping them with the techniques to get rid of their limiting beliefs and really achieve it just makes my heart sing. It really does.'

Jess and Gillian are helping women advocate for themselves and talk about formerly taboo subjects, like menopause, neurodiversity, parenting and money, in the workplace. Normalizing this starts to smooth out the obstacles, barriers and hurdles that employees from diverse backgrounds experience.

What unites these leaders

Porter's life mission, including all the businesses he's started and runs – from Jopwell that focuses on inclusive hiring, JodieAI which is building inclusive AI and 2045 Studio that helps companies create inclusive cultures – is about fixing what is fundamentally wrong with how organizations treat professionals of colour across the entire employee life cycle. Angie's mission is increasing female leadership in tech, Jess's is about opening space for women to talk about the full spectrum of their lives in the workplace and Gillian's is about empowering women to achieve their full potential. Lee's mission is to advocate for more inclusive working conditions for employees from the deaf and hard-of-hearing community. They are united by a powerful sense of purpose and their thoughtful and intentional use of language.

Porter says he is 'very cautious about language and words' in his leadership style. When he first started Jopwell at the age of 24, he felt he had to act like a CEO and believes he came across as unapproachable and intimidating. He says his priorities shifted when he became a parent for the first time, and since then he's become more approachable, honest and vulnerable. People mirror his actions: 'They're more receptive to ask for help. They are more receptive to talk about their vulnerability, where they feel insecure, things they need support on, rather than hiding things. They're open about it, and that allows us as a company to work through it, provide support, look at things differently.'

Porter's leadership philosophy mimics the Bridgewater approach. Bridgewater is an asset management firm, and its founder Ray Dalio created a flat structure based on a 'meritocracy of ideas.'[10] With this as his inspiration, Porter says debate is welcome in his company. 'If you have more experience in the thing than I do, then your opinion matters more than my opinion, no matter what my title says and what your title says. And we'll go with what you think.'

Still, he is the CEO, and people will act based on his words, so he ensures that he is very clear if something is just an opinion or a perspective or if it is a strongly held belief.

Angie's leadership communication style has also evolved. Her early experience in a male-dominated culture means she struggled to be authentic, but now she works on being authentic, human and vulnerable. She says there is no harm in over-communicating and keeps communication simple. 'Make sure you're clear on what your three key points are, and say them, say them and say them again.'

Angie is always thoughtful about using inclusive language. She says this is a continuous learning journey, not something you learn once and then you're done. 'I believe that all leaders should be educated on using inclusive language, but also be open to feedback as well, because often we will say things which used to be acceptable but fundamentally aren't now. It's about creating that psychological safety and that feedback loop so that we all learn and grow together,' she tells me.

Jess also talks about vulnerability, authenticity and honesty in her communication style. Although she uses the word authenticity several times, she says she's uncomfortable with it.

Jess says she learned from her father, who is a serial entrepreneur, that the onus of communication is on the transmitter. 'I've been brought up by someone who really knows the importance and value of thinking about your language in great depth. I try to choose my words carefully. I know that they can have a lasting impact. They can hurt or heal, and I always do my best to leave a positive impact on whatever I say and whoever I talk to.'

Gillian's neurodiversity plays a role in her communication style. She is 'sometimes all over the place with ideas' but has learned to turn this into a positive aspect in her client relationships:

'They've realized I was a bit different, in that I wasn't very corporate, and I was always more open and wanting to have fun with them. It's become part of the culture that people experience when they work with us. Now we put that into our bids and say we like to have fun with you. I think if you're going to work with clients, who have very serious culture change and problems and they're going to struggle to get people to turn up and they're going to get frustrated, they need someone to laugh with.'

Insight: Why is the idea of authenticity contested?

Early in my consulting career I had a conversation with a young LinkedIn influencer. I talked about how in my work it's important for me to help executives show up as their authentic selves. He made a face and said he hates the word authentic. His point was if you're saying you're authentic, you probably aren't. 'Just be real,' was his advice.

Why are we allergic to the idea of being authentic? There are several reasons.

Jess Rad says that authenticity has been 'gobbled up by commercialism' whether it's corporates showing their authentic face or influencers authentically selling us products.

It's possible that it's generational. We are a multi-generation and multi-cultural working population, all with different experiences of technology and how we function online. Younger people, like the LinkedIn influencer, are comfortable with knowing how they want to show up online: they're just real, no-one needs to coach them in how to be more human. Those of us who had to adjust to a more digital existence later in life have had to adapt. For executives used to being seen to be perfectly on top of everything they do, accepting a new way of being – slightly less scripted, slightly less perfect – is hard.

In *Let Them See You*, Porter shows that thanks to institutionalized racism and a fear of being misunderstood many people of colour feel unease at being their authentic selves at work.[11] He says, 'No matter how well you perform or how much recognition you receive, you won't achieve your full potential if you can't be who you are – who you *really* are – at work, day in and day out.'[12]

Being authentic at work is a way for leaders from diverse backgrounds to take back their power in a workplace that has a dominant leadership culture. For Porter, this is about knowing, understanding and internalizing your value.

When I posed this question on LinkedIn while writing the book, some of the commentators said that true authenticity is tied to having a clear purpose. If someone says something that is a mismatch to their values or purpose, we experience this as inauthentic. This goes back to the explanation of spin that we saw in Chapter 1 – if there's a gap, there's a problem; if you're explaining the gap the problem just got worse.

As we move towards a more transformative style of leadership, I'll continue to coach authenticity. Perfection is not relatable and being a bit fallible is fine as long as your internal values match your behaviour.

Communicating to build inclusive cultures

To address the inclusion gap, leaders and communicators need to work together to build an inclusive culture. Communications consultants Priya Bates and Advita Patel detail how in their book *Building a Culture of Inclusivity*. In it, they highlight the top five inclusive behaviours: asking powerful questions; being curious and asking for regular feedback; challenging poor behaviours and practices; creating a safe space for colleagues to speak up; and being aware of biases and assumptions.[13] One of their recommendations is to 'focus on the conversation, not the campaign.'[14]

In the interview with Shuchi Sharma, chief DEI officer of a US-based technology company with 20,000 employees, she told me that most of her job is about having conversations, whether one to one or in response to an internal crisis. She said a crisis arose during her first weeks and instead of getting to introduce herself she had to host a company-wide dialogue session:

> 'I invited the whole company to join and ask questions. Just learn. Ask questions, share your opinions. Let's have a dialogue, face to face, and that garnered so much positive feedback and support. People were so appreciative of the opportunity to share their experiences, and those that joined were so appreciative of the opportunity to learn.'

Language is key to building inclusive cultures. Researchers have shown that male-coded or agentic language in job descriptions send subtle signals to stereotypically masculine applicants. They found that: 'women felt that they were better fits, and were more interested in applying for, the jobs whose posts were high in communal language and low in agentic language.'[15]

Thoughts for allies

Those who do belong to the normative leadership demographic and want to help change leaders have three things to think about: inclusive language, inclusive behaviours and inclusive hiring. There are large numbers of resources out there on all these topics, but two places to start would be reading Priya's and Advita's book and listening to Porter's podcast. Educate yourself on how words exclude and consciously start to adapt less agentic and more communal language. Be highly conscious of how you hire, and – once you have hired someone from an URM into a leadership role – how you promote, remunerate, mentor and retain them. Ask for feedback from others on your own behaviour, try to accept advice graciously and demonstrate your willingness to learn and change. It takes vulnerability and self-awareness to do so.

Conclusion

DEI is complex, contested and multilayered. For companies and C-Suites to become truly diverse takes work, from leaders, managers and employees alike. As Lee's story shows, the inclusivity work never stops. Jess, Gillian and many others like them are helping individuals develop the courage to unlearn limiting beliefs and talk about subjects that have been previously taboo or swept under the carpet. The challenges of DEI are both contextual (trying to change a system that has been built over decades, which remains contested, and which continues to place obstacles in people's paths) and personal (finding the strength within to face down the obstacles and succeed despite them).

This chapter focused on four leaders who have founded businesses to help companies become more inclusive. They work in different ways: Porter is a highly visible serial founder whose focus is on building inclusivity for people of colour; Angie helps tech companies evolve their female leadership and talent retention; Gillian works to empower women; and Jess to help break taboos around topics that have been unspeakable in the workplace. All four are working within the context of systems and helping individuals. And all four are thoughtful and intentional about language and their leadership communication style.

Given that we know that organizational systems move slowly, and systemic change is hard to achieve, I'm interested to understand how diverse individuals break through despite the hurdles that exist – how they find leadership roles, how they keep them, how they build a progressive career and how they get to the C-Suite – and what commonalities exist.

From this chapter: Lessons in leadership communication

- CEOs don't have to be unapproachable and intimidating. People will mirror your actions, so be intentional in how you communicate.
- As a leader be very clear whether you are articulating an idea, a closely held belief or an instruction. People will act based on your words.
- Inclusive language is not a one-off lesson. You will have to keep learning. Don't be hard on yourself or on those who give you feedback.
- Make space in the workplace for difficult or previously taboo topics – this will help lighten the load your diverse employees carry.
- Accessibility is also inclusivity – don't create physical or technological hurdles for people with perceived disabilities.
- Conversations can be more effective than campaigns.
- Diversity is about much more than race and gender and can often be invisible.
- Leaders who wish to reshape the C-Suite need to work on building inclusive cultures, based on inclusive language, inclusive behaviours and inclusive hiring.

Chapter 3

Finding the leader within – landing or creating a dream job

Leadership is evolving. Just as we are (slowly) learning not to equate loud confidence with leadership competence, we are also learning to accept different kinds of leadership. The interviewees in this book ranged from CEOs, senior managers and founders to people in their first management roles and people who work solo. All identify as leaders.

Leadership is not a job title. It does not mean complying with a norm or mirroring the leaders around us. It may mean leading a team and having direct reports, and it may not. It may mean climbing the career ladder and following a linear path to the top job, and it may not. It may mean working alone as a fractional CFO with a portfolio of different customers. It may mean being a founder, working alone with occasional freelance support.

As a society, we are obsessed with thinking and talking about leadership, and those who lead. If you go into any bookshop, the shelves are lined with books on leadership. Entire university departments are devoted to the theory and study of leadership. Experts like Simon Sinek and Adam Grant have huge social media followings based on their leadership research, writing and podcasts. This shows how curious we are.

It's not my goal to define leadership here, but it is my goal to shine a light on ways we can change it. The question I'm trying to answer is: How do we get from a leadership cohort that is still predominantly a monoculture to one that is more diverse?

I decided to learn from leaders themselves. And in this chapter, I reflect on some of the lessons I learned from emerging leaders – those who are new to it, who come from a wide range of backgrounds and who are finding their feet in an early leadership role.

Lessons from emerging diverse leaders

Katja Kolmetz is the founder and CEO of a company called Wavemakers. Having had corporate roles in her early twenties where she felt she was trying to meet the expectations of others, Katja was inspired to find a way of leading that was comfortable to her. She describes this as trying to find a way to lead 'where I didn't have to put on a mask and try to be someone I was not.' And having found that, Katja and her Wavemakers team have built a company to help the next generation find leadership inside themselves. They now have a community of 15,000 young professionals around the globe and Katja is regularly invited to give keynotes and speak on panels about a new kind of leadership.

Interrogate the leadership stereotype

Thinking of leadership stereotypes as men versus women is reductive. Katja says:

> 'I realized that it's not about women or men but that there are many people who are different from the current leadership stereotype that we have in our minds. We're constantly navigating this idea of changing ourselves to fit in – or being different, and then not being fully valued or respected for it.'

Either way, this causes discomfort. New leaders are either trying to fit into a mould that doesn't sit well with them or challenging it entirely. Katja says emerging leaders often articulate their challenges as if there is something wrong with them. They feel the need to change something about who they are to fit in.

Katja believes there is another way, and this is the basis of Wavemakers' mission to redefine leadership.

> 'It takes a lot of courage and strength to break some of these patterns and create change. You can't expect everyone to do that, but if some people gain that perspective and gain that energy to poke some holes into the idea of what makes a perfect leader professional, they start to see it in themselves.'

Finding (a new kind of) leadership within

John Alexander became the youngest city councillor ever in Dundee, Scotland, at the age of 23. He was invited to stand for the Scottish National Party in 2012 while still at university. John's motivation was not so much a love of politics itself but a strong compunction that Dundee needed politicians that resembled the area.

John grew up in a working-class family. His father never spent a day out of work, taking up new roles when other work dried up to make ends meet, his mother escaped domestic violence in the 1980s fleeing to Dundee, and his brother spent time in jail as a teenager (importantly, after finishing his term: gaining qualifications, attending university, getting married and building a positive life). John explains that he has always been extremely honest about his background in interviews and conversations:

> 'I think this helps me in my job because I've got a bit of a deeper understanding what people feel and see and how their lives interact with reality. It also helps because people know you're not bullshitting.
>
> Going into different conversations with constituents and being able to say I might not exactly understand how

you feel but here's what happened to me opens up avenues of conversation. But it also means that I get a really honest reflection of what's going on in Dundee, which means I can do my job better. I am brutally honest with people about my own experiences but also what I perceive.'

John translated that brutal honesty into a 12-year political career. He was never the politician who made big promises. Instead, he focused his language on how problems would be tackled, and his strategies were emulated in other Scottish districts.

Reflecting on leadership, John says those who excel are those who are true to themselves:

'And they've always been the ones that don't require other people to help them with momentum, drive, determination or focus. They have a crystal-clear vision of what they want to achieve, how they want to achieve that and who they want to achieve it for.'

A few months after our interview, John announced he was standing down from his many political roles (leader of Dundee City Council, chair of the Scottish Cities Alliance, co-chair of a Poverty Commission and deputy chair of the Climate Leadership Commission). In the announcement he said the balance between being a good father and husband and an effective council leader was becoming harder to manage.

In a way he predicted this when he talked about being one of the first councillors ever to take paternity leave:

'There shouldn't be barriers. We should be enabling people from all walks of life to get involved, but we need to support them. We need to challenge structures, and we need to change them. Because if nothing changes, then we'll never get those people coming to the fore in terms of the roles and responsibilities that they could excel in. I've seen really good people, exceptional leaders, leave jobs because structures are preventing them from being all that they could be – and is actually only to the detriment of the organization, not to that individual.'

Leading from outside the hierarchy

Another emerging leader I interviewed who is driven by purpose and challenging structures is Musema Robert, a Ugandan fashion designer who runs an avant-garde social activism fashion brand called Msema Culture. He designs and makes all the clothes himself and has three full-time and several part-time employees. He is also deeply connected with his local community, where he trains women and girls in sewing skills to help them find work and create income. His products also serve to communicate something to the community where he lives and works, and the last collection for men and women celebrated a narrative around menstrual rights and menstrual hygiene.

Musema says his drive to help women and highlight women's issues comes from his very close relationship to his mother, who, on her own, worked to ensure that he had the tuition fees for school and university.

He's proud of the number of people he has mentored in his community. He currently has ten women in an 18-month programme and in total has mentored over 60 women. The skills they learn aren't restricted to sewing. 'I also teach them how to make liquid soap, because this is something they can learn in one week and then start selling their product right away.' The women also learn tailoring and how to make reusable pads. Once women have graduated from the programme he helps them to find jobs with other organizations, but his dream is to grow his own business enough so that he can hire more people.

He feels his leadership has been challenged by the fact that he does not look like a typical leader in a suit and tie. The idea of diversity, and different kinds of leaders who are not typical, is only just arriving in Uganda. He found it very hard to get into leadership programmes because he is a young Black person with dreadlocks. (However, he was able to join WaveMakers which helped him with many things, including leadership and communication skills, as well as other business skills including tips on technology.)

Musema identifies as culturally Rastafarian, and he appreciates that the Rastafari way has helped him in the promotion of peace and love, community building, social justice and activism as well as doing awareness programmes. It helps him to be a leader in his community even if he does not have a title because 'if you work to shape the community, you are a leader.'

He sees leadership as being outside a hierarchy or a job, but rather something that grows out of passion:

> 'So, for us, we take it to be something that's just free. You do it on your own at your will. You do it with passion, because that's the best thing that we can do. Being a leader with passion without the hierarchies and the ranks, so that you are not compromised.'

The idea of leading from outside the hierarchy was confirmed by another interviewee, Lara Heskestad, who works in a multilateral organization focused on international development. Throughout her experience across multicultural settings, she came to realize that rather than taking on an active, front-facing leadership role, she preferred to lead and influence from the side, as she calls it:

> 'My superpower is being able to observe what is going on in the room, seeing the impact of what the leader says and the way they lead on people. If there is a disconnect, I try to identify the source and then use empathy and communication

to bridge the gap. By leading from the side, I'm able to be effective, influence change in organizations and help others achieve their goals in a way that feels most natural to me.'

Non-linear, non-traditional, no fear

Preeti Shetty is the only South Asian woman on the board of a Premier League football club. Overall, only 10% of Premier League football club board members are women. As a child growing up in Dubai to Indian parents, she played and watched sport, but never planned to make it her career. After studying media and communications in the UK, she landed an internship at BBC Sport where she realized two things: first, that sport is all about storytelling; and second, that it has the potential to change lives. 'You start to realize that the inequity that exists in society is extremely visible in sport. And so, you start to break down what that is like for women and girls, what that is like for women of colour, and people with disabilities.'

That interest in measuring data plays out in her role as CEO of Upshot, a social enterprise that measures the impact of nonprofit sports organizations.

Preeti's route to CEO was not traditional. After finishing work at the BBC, she did a Masters in sports management and wrote her thesis on monitoring evaluation tools in sport for the development sector. One of these tools was Upshot, which the Football Foundation (FF) was in the process of launching. After her masters, she began working for the FF on their Upshot launch and in 2016 she became head of Upshot. In 2021, Preeti bought Upshot from the FF and became the owner.

The process of running Upshot – while simultaneously buying it from the FF – was not easy for Preeti and the team. They had to find a lot of money fast, and she had to manage the transition from being an employee to being an owner.

And it's not about a linear career. She has 'a lot of side hustles' and she encourages her team to do the same:

'I tell them, it will make you better at this job and it'll make you less fearful and less dependent if this goes wrong. That's where we stifle innovation is when we put the fear of God in people that they can't fail. I think that's what I'm most proud of: that I'm not scared to fail.'

As the CEO of Upshot, a board member for Brentford and holding several other board positions, Preeti is now recognized as a campaigner and spokesperson for social justice through sport.

How emerging leaders land their dream jobs is as different as the leaders themselves. How do they think about how they communicate?

Identity, leadership and communication

Preeti believes that her identity has shaped who she is as a leader:

'And as I've got older, it's shaped my communications style. When I first came to this country, I would very rarely talk about identity, gender or ethnicity. It was about fitting in. Whereas now I am much more comfortable in my own skin, and I realize it's the edge. I would never have said that as a woman of colour ten years ago. But I recognize the power it has now.'

Preeti is clear that identity can sometimes get in the way. For her, it can feel like an emotional burden when other people bring it up. 'I'm here to talk about something and actually all you want to talk about is my experience. And so, I think that balance is very delicate. When you can take ownership of it but not feel forced into it.'

Representation still matters. And since women of colour aren't represented enough in sport and on boards, she will continue to talk about her identity. However, her advice to others is you own your identity. You get to choose when you want to talk about your experience, and you get to say when you think it's not relevant.

In terms of communications, Preeti says she is a great external communicator as she's had a lot of external speaking opportunities. She is not as good at internal communications because she forgets that not everyone in her team communicates in terms of ideas the way she does. Since they are a young team and the business is moving so fast, how they communicate with each other is constantly shifting.

Preeti would be liked to be known for always wanting to help and wanting to break down the barriers, 'for having purpose, and for building a community that helps each other.'

Use of language

Musema is thoughtful about how he communicates but believes it's not only about delivering a message – it's about how the audience perceives it. 'And that's why at times we've got feedback from our audience to see whether the communication that we're issuing is received in the way we want it to be. Or it's understood in the way that we want it to be.'

He thinks deeply about the words he uses and the effect they may have, because words can be emotional.

In terms of her leadership communication, Katja is aware of how she communicates to her team and the outside world. She believes in honesty and in meaningful communication, but she is also aware that her words carry weight, so she chooses them carefully. She is aware of this as a leadership responsibility. Working in an environment where most people are non-native English, including herself, she focuses on clarity of language.

Also, communication for Katja is not only about sending out words but about having an exchange. When she's speaking in public, she tries to read the audience, and to respond to their feedback spontaneously.

Katja is thoughtful about language and about her leadership style. Her personal interpretation of diversity and inclusion means she is always listening to different perspectives and evaluating them. She gave me an example of a leadership communication issue where an employee asked her to make a stand on social media on a particular topic, and how, after asking many people's opinions and checking her own biases, she decided she would not and explained her decision carefully to the staff member. 'It's not about having ego, or enforcing my opinion, but about a two-way collaboration in which different perspectives surface, and then we make a decision based on what is best for the business.'

She says while this is a continuous effort, this is how they create the best outcomes and make the best progress. This kind of collaboration also leads to employee satisfaction and retention.

Another leader who is very thoughtful about their communication style is Rishabh Gupta, who leads the data science team at a tech company in the UK. His parents are Indian, and he grew up in Kuwait. The family fled back to India during the war, where Rishabh studied and began his early career. After working in consulting for a few years, including in Dubai, he founded a start-up, which he had to mothball after a few years. After that, he decided to further his education and did an MBA in Spain. He is now married and lives and works in the UK.

Rishabh describes himself as an outsider – when growing up in Kuwait, when he returned to India and now in the UK. And it is these layers of experience, what he describes as 'a sum of many things' – including his acknowledgement of being an introvert – that inform how he communicates as a leader now.

'I've been someone who's an outsider, and because I've been someone who's not a local or not feeling at home, in many ways, I tend to make sure that other people are aware and are comfortable,' he says. Making sure others are aware means that he is unafraid to ask what he calls 'the stupid questions.' Working in other cultures means he hasn't always understood slang or turns of phrase. He will always ask for clarification, not because he wants to put the speaker on the spot, but because he wants to ensure that other people don't feel uncomfortable. He's always aiming for clarity.

Rishabh tends towards empathy in his leadership communication. He always wants to understand where people are coming from, and he likes to keep things simple. If he senses there's confusion, he will call a team member and clarify things in a personal conversation.

He also invites his team to give feedback. 'Every quarter, we'll reflect on how we work as a team,' he says. This gives his team the chance to speak openly about changes, confirm what is working and how they can meet their goals.

Another thoughtful communicator is David Nath, who runs a large team of data analysts, engineers and scientists at a company in Berlin, Germany. David identifies as first-generation immigrant, queer, non-binary and neurodiverse. They grew up in India, where with their aptitude for science, they were expected to study engineering. However, they were convinced that statistics was going to be important in the world where data-related topics such as computer science were rapidly evolving. They did a BSc statistics in Kolkata, followed by a masters in statistics at University College, Dublin.

After university, they began working at KPMG Ireland. One of the conditions of the job was getting the Chartered Accountants qualification, which they did.

Growing up in India, David was bullied for being different. But it was only when they started attending diversity and inclusion events at KPMG, and eventually representing Ireland on the DEI global forum, that they found the self-esteem, courage and support to come out. David says they realized co-leading DEI for KPMG Global that:

> 'this is what I am good at. I can bring my experience. I can bring my own perspective. And I was really surprised to see that they listened to my ideas, and this inculcated with me a great sense of self-esteem. I realized that I bring a lot of fresh, great ideas to people. And also, that people look up to me.'

David says one of the biggest challenges they face in their career is 'sometimes accepting to go into places where I may not be happy, or where people might challenge me.' Having always been a people pleaser, it's sometimes hard to deal with the fact that, now they're presenting as their full self, sometimes people might criticize or have negative opinions about them. However, they consider their biggest career success that they decided to go into a new workplace presenting as nonbinary, without asking what the HR policies were.

They said they knew in that moment there was no way that they were going to ask other people how they should act. And if you think back to the authenticity discussion in the last chapter, this is the ultimate authentic act: showing up as you are without asking for permission.

Not asking for permission

Asked about how their identity intersects with their leadership, David says the more intersectional you are and the fewer privileges you have, the more resilience and empathy you have. This showed up when they were giving quarterly feedback to a team member about being neurodiverse in the workplace. They told this person that the more resistance you face, the more problem-solving skills you develop. This team member told them they were a mentor to them.

'I brought a lot of my intersectionality with me, the resilience, the resistance and the empathy, and transferred these skills to another person.'

Language is important to David. In a work environment where people come from so many language backgrounds, they try to always understand people's intention.

As a leader, David tries to communicate in a clear way and has put a lot of effort into improving their English and their business communication. They also try not to be defensive and will always try to sit down with someone and have a conversation to clear the air. They have learned effective communication (talk about the event, talk about your feelings, talk about your need, and then end with the wish) and when asking for feedback, they always ask for examples. Their biggest learning in leadership communication is 'I can acknowledge your feelings, and I acknowledge my feelings, but I do not take responsibility for your feelings.'

They believe they have learned to be a good leader, although they say leadership is as much about the perception of others as it is about having a management position. 'You cannot just say that you are a leader, you also need to be perceived as a leader.'

This is one of the core principles of reputation, which we'll focus on in Part 2. Shortly after our interview, David was promoted by their company and is now managing a large team. David's effectiveness in the role and their empathetic communication style has led to their recognition.

Advice to emerging leaders

Porter Braswell's book *Let Them See You* is a great collection of real-world strategies for overcoming obstacles in the workplace. While it addresses people of colour, it is completely relevant for anyone whose identities are not of the norm, or who face hurdles in landing and building their dream leadership jobs.

I highlight some strategies here because they are tied to building a reputation, or demonstrating your value at work (what Katja Kolmetz calls 'externalizing your value').

Porter says a 'critical mistake that many young professionals make, especially to those new to an organization, is waiting until their annual review to highlight their achievements.'[1] Highlight your achievements early and often to stay visible. He also recommends that people of diverse identities track everything (including training, information you sought from people outside your department, extra hours worked, collaborations and anything you initiated) and update this list weekly. I would add that it's important to articulate to yourself how these helped you support and drive company strategy, so you link your behaviour to strategy.

He devotes a chapter to building your personal brand, both inside the company and online, and another to becoming and remaining your authentic self. As we will see in the section on reputation both the stories you tell about yourself, and the way you behave are key to building a long-lasting reputation.

Conclusion

This chapter focused on six emerging leaders – one politician, two founders, one CEO and two senior managers. The idea of a leadership role is different for everyone, but there are several common factors. Everyone has struggled and felt on the outside of something. Each has had to dig deep, acknowledge truths about themselves, and use those truths to fuel their passion for taking the next career step, whatever it might be.

All of them see language as a powerful tool and use it thoughtfully. They are aware of language nuances and where they need to get better at using it.

From this chapter: Lessons in leadership communication

- Emerging leaders are breaking accepted patterns of what professional and what leadership look like.
- Their careers can be non-linear, or they accept leadership roles early in their careers.
- They are not asking for permission for how they show up in the workplace.
- They are thoughtful about language, considerate in how they communicate and empathetic about how what they say is received.
- Representation matters but individuals get to choose when and how they articulate their identity or diverse background.
- They are skipping the traditional hierarchy and building work based on passion.
- Leadership is as much as being perceived as a leader by others as it is about having a management position.

Chapter 4

Finding the right culture – keeping a dream job

Senior leaders have experience on their side. They've worked in several companies and they have resumes with depth. However, diverse leaders also have to pick and choose their companies carefully. Some company cultures are just not a great fit, no matter the promises made at the outset.

Having a good leadership reputation is key to getting a leadership role, but keeping one is a different story. In a leadership monoculture, I want to understand how leaders from underrepresented minorities (URM) get their dream jobs and keep them, how they bolster themselves against microaggressions and other workplace challenges, and how they lead for longevity.

In Chapter 1, I talked about context (the crisis of leaders) and behaviour (the crisis for leaders). In one leader's journey, the different workplaces they enter will provide the context, which is largely out of their control. They can control how they lead and communicate. If the context and their behaviour match, they will build longevity in that company, but if the two become too disparate, they might leave.

I spoke to several CEOs, C-Suite and senior leaders about the intersection of reputation, leadership and diversity to find out how they try to ensure the match works – and how reputation can help in the interplay of finding and keeping the dream leadership role.

Lessons from senior leaders from diverse backgrounds

Tania Pemberton is a senior sales leader in the UK. Until recently, she was director of sales for an educational information service provider based in the US, and responsible for business of £40 million, with 14 direct reports. Between the births of her two children, she was promoted to a manager role. After her second child was born, she asked her managers if she could start a new job as an individual contributor in a different part of the business (in other words, to step down from being a manager) because she was getting bored and wanted a new challenge:

> 'It was specifically to do with schools, colleges and public libraries and I wanted the challenge of doing something new. I thought I could make a real difference to that market. But it wasn't a management role. And they wouldn't let me do it. They wouldn't let me take a step down. They said you're overqualified, and you'll never improve your career.'

Non-linear can be the most direct route

After threatening to leave, Tania was allowed to take on the new role, which she did for three years, elevating it to a two-million-pound business. She was then promoted to a senior management role with several employees, responsible for a multi-million-pound sales budget. The non-linear step, which was highly disapproved of by Tania's management, was the fuel for a much more senior role with a higher profit and loss responsibility and a global team. This shows that a non-linear career can be very creative and jumpstart something new and unexpected.

However, in Tania's case the culture did not approve, and she had to go to the step of threatening to leave before she was allowed to make the side-step.

A career with longevity will have fits and starts and some rerouting. A job that looks ideal might not be; taking a longer way around might be the shortest route. Tania followed her instinct, and her instinct was to take a role where she would learn the most.

Creating the culture you don't see

Culturally, the company wasn't an ideal fit for her: 'It was definitely the suit and tie, old boys' network kind of place, although they were trying to change that.'

She says there was one female leader in the organization who could be a role model for her, but that person did not have children. Tania was the only leader with primary childcare responsibilities. Her peers either had no children, much older children or had a stay-at-home primary parent caring for their children. Looking back, Tania now says she 'just dealt with it,' but in essence this meant getting up hours earlier than her colleagues, getting children ready for and to school, a long commute, working a full day, commuting, then taking the children to their after-school activities, feeding them and starting again the next day. She says her car became her second office, because she'd sit in it writing emails. This is the parent tax, and it usually lands on female leaders.

Seeing the lack of diversity in the hierarchy above her made Tania very conscious about hiring for diversity and hers was the most diverse team in the organization:

'Diversity of thought adds value to a team dynamic. We were working in a sales environment, and it was very much if you keep doing the same thing, you're going to get the same results. I was always very keen to make sure that we could look for different ways of doing things. And one way of doing that is having diverse people who can think more creatively and who apply their knowledge from one industry to another.'

Tania also says being menopausal at the same time as leading a large team with big financial goals was not always easy:

'There was never an open forum where you could say, you know what, brain fog is quite a challenge, or I haven't slept very well. So, I think encouraging people to perhaps be slightly more open is important, because that's how we change the organizations. If we acknowledge it, then they must start dealing with it. If we try and mask or pretend it's not happening then it's our problem, not theirs.'

While Tania was operating in a culture that was not an ideal fit for her, she created a great culture within her own team. This is a response I see often with senior leaders – they ensure that their teams embody the culture they would like to see across the whole organization – and something I also worked on when leading a global team.

The joy of being a senior leader is that you have a corner of the organization where you can create a pocket of culture that serves you and your team well. The downside of this is while you might create psychological safety, that might not exist outside your team boundaries, so then you need to work on creating resilience so that people can cope. This might result in team members feeling split, divided and uncomfortable.

Another leader who responded to a particular corporate culture by creating something of her own is Vuyi M'Cwabeni. She lives in Germany and hails from an immigrant background (she is Zimbabwean born, with both South African and Canadian citizenship). After working in strategy and services in a technology company, Vuyi was promoted to chief of staff and head of global product strategy under the board member in charge of a 20,000-person department.

When her new job was announced internally in the company – as one of a handful of very senior people of colour – Vuyi was taken aback by the outpouring of support:

> 'I did not realize how many other people needed to see me there. I was truly shocked because I compared myself unfavourably to all the other very senior guys, but people said you have no idea how important it is to us. I started to understand how role models matter, how important it is for people to be able to see someone like them in a senior role.'

As a woman and person of colour in a prominent leadership role, Vuyi says she tried to tell herself the narrative that race did not matter, and she was there on her own merits. She said another senior leader who was both male and white told her: 'You can go very, very high. But you have to be very careful because the grip of this constellation means they will let you fall very, very far if you're not really smart about how you manage your career.'

From that moment on, she was aware that as a woman she needed to be extra smart but also extra careful. And as a Black person, she needed to be extra resilient. Vuyi describes always carrying this double awareness, while also succeeding in a pressurized job, as 'a weight.'

This is the context of a culture that is not completely welcoming to those who present differently from the norm. In addition, she says her experience of the culture in the company was that it put people last, had no transparency, was suffering from intellectual stagnation and too much homogeneity.

Later in her career, when Vuyi founded a fintech company with two other founders she focused strongly on building a culture in which people could thrive: 'We set out to build a culture characterized by a deep commitment to empathy (one of our brand archetypes was the caregiver), ethical integrity, continuous learning, and inclusivity.'

After banking regulations changed in Germany and a tough funding climate, Vuyi and her co-founders were forced to shutter the company. She is now pursuing a solo career as a board advisor, strategist and public speaker. When we last spoke, she told me she is also taking on the CEO role for an early-stage IT software company and has co-founded a Korean beauty skin care line. 'The idea is to just keep on having fun,' she said.

Insight: Investing in ways others don't have to

I'm Gen X – the generation of women who were told we could be anything we wanted to be. Our mothers, who were housewives, secretaries, nurses and teachers, were ambitious for us. We stepped into corporate roles and were just as ambitious, confident and determined as our male counterparts. However, as soon as we became parents (or even before) the setbacks arrived: discrimination, salary freezes, the inability to progress in our careers. Some of us responded by stepping out of the workplace altogether, others took part-time jobs, others juggled madly in senior roles as Tania describes. This is more than the parent tax – it's the motherhood tax.

And when we did stay in work, and aim for senior roles, then we experienced criticism of how we did or did not parent. Vuyi says that many of her German and mostly male colleagues found it difficult to understand why and how she managed to continue working full-time with two small children. She found herself continually having to explain or justify her decision. She had to invest in childcare to manage her full-time leadership role, and while her managers saw her commitment to her job, they struggled to understand her motivation.

In my own case, I had to send my children to a fee-paying school with afterschool care to be able to manage working full-time, and still I had managers question my commitment to my job.

Investing in yourself

A leader who articulates the struggle to fit into the context of a culture very ably is Meg Bear, now a board member and advisor whose last role was as president of a software division in a tech company. Meg is a fifth generation native of San Francisco's Bay Area, and the first person in her whole family to go to university. Having built a successful progressive career in technology with several leadership roles, she describes herself as a class immigrant.

Meg says she joined tech as an outsider, and so for the first few years never thought of herself as a 'woman in tech.' She spent so much time being the youngest in the room that it took her a while to realize she was also the only woman in the room. She got her first job in 1992 which: 'was a moment where in the US we perceived that there was a lot of opportunity for women, so it just never really occurred to me that there was anything as a barrier because of my gender.'

It was only once she worked in larger organizations in leadership roles where she started to see that she was not being taken as seriously as some of her peers. Her instinct was just to work harder, but even that wasn't making the difference she expected. She realized she was going to have to invest in ways that others didn't:

'I need to build a different strategy. Because this package, this body, this set of experiences is going to face a certain set of barriers that are different and therefore I need to find additional ways around those barriers. So, it unlocked innovation in my own thinking of seeing that this is another hurdle with unspoken and unwritten rules that I need to figure out and navigate.'

Amplified emotional intelligence

Ernesto Marinelli is the board member responsible for people and culture at a European property company. He has spent much of his career in tech and found himself in leadership by chance. His ambition growing up in a small village near Rome was to be a professor, but when studying linguistics in Germany, a friend told him he was good at networking and should consider HR.

Ernesto feels that living in Germany as a gay man and an immigrant has amplified his emotional intelligence. He had the feeling that as a 'second-class citizen' he had to prove himself twice but was always lucky to find leaders who supported him. In terms of his own leadership, he started to become aware that people appreciated his support and how he made them feel.

Before he became a manager, he started to realize that he could influence people's lives without having authority. He says:

> 'That was also an interesting part of my career, where I could combine building trust, emotional intelligence, empathy, with a sense of compassion for others. That helped me, and I had the impression that the teams in the countries were calling me to ask me if I needed help proactively. This was the moment in which I realized this is a differentiating element in the way I relate to people.'

Tania agrees. She believes that her identity intersects with her leadership communications style in that she tends to nurture team members, show empathy and focus on being positive. 'I always think about maximizing the potential in somebody, which probably comes from my teaching background. And that goes for my customers as well as my direct reports.'

The value of neutral communication

In terms of her leadership communication, Tania says she employed skills she learned in her coaching courses – active listening, asking questions, building trust. She also took care of her team members in a very personal way, understanding what was happening in their personal lives 'especially during Covid.'

Coaching also helped her be aware of her language use as a leader. She focused on using clean language, a coaching concept which aims to improve communication and avoid misunderstanding by avoiding influencing people's thoughts and responses with emotive words:

> 'If it was an important conversation, I would definitely be cautious of what I was saying. I was also consciously, quite positive because if you're dealing with difficult situations, it's best not to brush them under the carpet, but to find some positive learning or some kind of positive element from the experience.'

Tania says she can be quite direct and focus on the headlines, and that leadership taught her about focusing on details. She would adapt this according to the person she was talking to:

> 'Some people like a lot of detail, so I would force myself to talk about detail. I'd much prefer just to talk about sort of big picture stuff. On a team of 14, you've got 14 very different personalities. And they all need and want slightly different things. And I think being able to adapt your style, certainly in a one to one, I think is massively important.'

Don't rein yourself in

Vuyi advises people to not feel forced to rein in their personalities. 'I was boxed in and told to make myself smaller, and I had to unlearn that.' This is so important, and something many senior leaders need to unlearn. Emerging leaders seem to be more in touch with who they are and how they show up at work. It's my contention that the vast coaching industry is helping leaders of my generation unlearn the lessons of making oneself smaller. Be who you are at work, don't ask permission, don't make yourself small.

She says it takes time to hone your individual voice but finding it can be a career game changer. She also advises people to find their communication sweet spot. Some are great on stage in front of 10,000 people; others are better in a small room. She says the work is about finding out where you shine and maximizing that.

Address microaggressions

Mona heads the EMEA analyst relations team at a large software company. We spoke shortly after the explosion of right-wing violence in the UK in the summer of 2024. As a person who is Muslim, Black and a woman, Mona says it's 'a trifecta when I come along.' She also identifies as someone from a Somali background, a working parent and a mother of a neurodiverse child.

One of the things she does very consciously at work is counteract microaggressions with education:

> 'I'm not confrontational, but I will call someone up after I witness something and let them know. I like to have those conversations on the side, because it's about educating the person, because they may say something that is not necessarily correct or maybe not be taken in the right way.'

Mona says this type of conversation is powerful because it allows the person to talk through where they were actually coming from: 'Maybe not as a bad place as you would think when actually communicating right verbally, or they've used the wrong words. So, it's just about getting to an understanding and helping them to think twice next time.'

Another leader who uses personal conversations to address micro-aggressions is Kholi, whom we first heard from in Chapter 1. The youngest in a family of ten children, a single mother, sole breadwinner, and a chartered accountant with a storied career at various multinational companies, she describes what it was like being promoted above four male peers:

> 'It was quite difficult, because men want to show their dominance, that they know better. And my approach was after one meeting, where one was dominating. I asked him to stay on after a meeting. He said, "I didn't mean to disrespect you", and I said you need to understand why I was appointed. I have these qualities, this CV, these credentials and this set of expertise. I think from that day, it changed our relationship, because now he understood why I was selected.'

Foster curiosity

In her leadership communications, Meg likes to foster curiosity and spark ideas. She'll use channels like LinkedIn or Slack to drop breadcrumbs for people to ponder and navigate. She also enjoys larger-scale communications, like hosting an all-hands meeting, when 'there's a real need and time and place for that. And to me it's not just about what you say but about the energy that you bring.' On a smaller scale, she enjoys getting to know people individually and understanding what makes them tick:

> 'I love creating enthusiasm within someone to take something on that they might not believe that they're quite ready for. So in in that regard, I love figuring out what is that motivator for someone that unlocks their potential, gets them out of their own fear zone and into challenging themselves.'

In terms of language and how she uses it, Meg tries to communicate without pretence:

'I don't take myself too seriously and my teams know I don't take myself too seriously. My role is not figurehead. My role is a member of the mission team, and I care a lot about using language that makes it clear that life is short, and I enjoy a little bit of whimsy and a little bit of levity. I'm not super interested in pomp and circumstance.'

When she has communication challenges or bad news to impart, Meg errs on the side of radical candour. She might get advice from her communications teams for help with tonality, but she really wants people to believe she is being straight with them. 'And in order for that to be the case, I need to be straight with them.'

She likes to open space for people to ask her why something is happening in the business, and for that, her favourite way to communicate is via a Q&A session. She says the way people ask a question gives her a lot of information about where they are, how they are feeling and what their narrative is, which she can then acknowledge in her responses. She does the same thing when she's reading the comments from a culture survey: trying to understand the emotion behind the words, and the language respondents use to understand their context better.

Appreciation for multiple perspectives

Meg says it's hard to separate her identity from her leadership communication because lived experience and professional experience are intertwined. As someone who has often been an outsider, she has a deeper appreciation for the idea that there are multiple perspectives than she thinks others do. She also thinks she has a:

'much deeper curiosity for figuring out how to build connection authentically, not to change who I am, because it's not my goal to become something that's more palatable for others, but to help people understand who I am better so that we can together figure out how to work together best.'

She feels it's hard to separate that core outsider experience from the value she's able to create because she knows what it's like to think differently. Meg compares being an outsider to the immigrant experience: 'When people have had to pick up and change country or change culture, which was just a super big shock to the system. There are just certain things that don't play the same here as they do there.'

Having that set of tools has allowed her to build connection with people and is usefully different from others' tools:

'Because the most important part of building connection is to figure out authentically who you are and to figure out how to build that shared understanding and I have been blessed to have built some additional tools in this area because of the context of how I came to them.'

Because of where she's come from, Meg says she's had a bigger barrier to get through and has had to work harder to build credibility. 'I understand already I have more work to do' (than others). This speaks again to the barriers and obstacles that leaders from URM minorities face in the workplace. However, once you build credibility as a leader, you then have more power.

Advocacy – in terms of advocating for others – is important, especially when, as a leader, you have reached a position of power and privilege. For Meg, advocacy 'is action-based, but it's also a lot about being visible and taking up space in general. And then taking action, as in when there are opportunities, when you have the power or the position to change the conversation or to create opportunity for others.'

Thinking about her reputation as a leader, Meg says it's very important to be seen and known as a whole person:

> 'The more of a leadership role you have, the bigger the set of audiences that are watching you, it's important that you don't just try to develop a persona but that you remind everyone yourself included, of the humanity of it all. You can be very smart and powerful and also a little bit of a hot mess and have bad days, and that retains the connective tissue with the people you're leading. I care about people seeing me as a full human not as just an archetype.'

Insight: Be fully human, not an archetype

I love this lesson from Meg, which speaks to the authenticity discussion in Chapter 2. Leaders who have personas are hard to relate to and unreachable. We are not consumer products, no matter how polished our profiles, and showing up as fully human makes us relatable. It also speaks to the inherent perfectionism in being an archetype.

One of the things I learned recently was about single and double-loop learning. Researchers discovered that corporate leaders were bad at learning, because they were single-loop learners – their goal was to solve the problem and then move on. Double-loop learners ask, 'what role did I play in causing the problem? How does my solution reinforce the problem?'

Leaders who are single-loop learners are also likely to have a persona of perfection as a self-protection tool. It's much more human to say 'hey, I made a mistake, how can I learn from this?'

Jeffrey Pfeffer, Stanford University professor and author of *Power*, says that slight non-perfection can help when looking for a dream leadership role. He says, 'strategically put out enough negative but not fatally damaging information about yourself that the people who hire and support you fully understand any weaknesses and make the choice anyway.'[1]

Using informal communication

As a senior leader, Ernesto says in times of change there is no such thing as over-communicating. While he follows all the formal channels (team meetings, announcements, emails and so on), he also calls people on his team spontaneously to find out how they are doing and what they need. He says this informal communication is more important because it is where people open up to him. He is thoughtful in terms of his use of language, especially as he is mostly communicating in his third language (English).

Reputation is important – his, that of his team and of the company. Ernesto says reputation is like putting on a nice, ironed shirt (instead of one that you wore for 30 days). It has a huge impact. When he first arrived in his new role, from a large global company to a smaller one, he produced white papers for his team on important topics such as learning and development. This gave them a reference point and a deeper understanding that helped them communicate to others in a broader way. The goal of this exercise was to improve their communication skills and be able to represent the company with deeper knowledge.

He feels his identity is core to who he is as a human being. And as a gay man, he never stops coming out, so he is always weighing the impact on others when he tells them his spouse is a man. He feels it is right to explain, and he always does, but he is aware that it has an effect.

Ernesto sees leadership as much more than steps on a ladder. 'It has many facets, in which we influence each other outside or despite the hierarchy.' He sees a 'democratization of leadership,' which means we lead even when we do not manage a team. This is underscored by social media, in which we can lead by sharing our thoughts and opinions in a positive way to always improve our environment.

Conclusion

The leadership priorities have shifted. Both emerging and senior leaders are highly conscious of how they are perceived and how they impact others. Emerging leaders have done personal work on themselves and lead in a humane way. Senior leaders measure their words and their impact on others carefully.

Leaders are thoughtful about how they use words because they are intentional about making meaning for others. All of the actions they describe – self-awareness, thoughtful use of language, creating meaning for others, opening space for others, being mentors, addressing microaggressions, innovating themselves, being messy – feed into their reputation equity. Words matter. Combined with consistent action, they are the building blocks of a leader's reputation.

From this chapter: Lessons in leadership communication

- There is no shame in a non-linear career – it can be the most direct route.
- Don't work on being palatable or an archetype; enjoy showing up as fully human, and yourself.
- Become a double-loop learner: ask yourself and acknowledge what your role was in creating a problem.
- Address microaggressions in the spirit of learning not shaming.
- Create the culture you want to see in your own team.

Part 2

New relationship metrics

To manage and mitigate reputational risk, CEOs need to build a relationship of trust with their Chief Communications Officer. The context of their work is reputational – for the company and for the CEO. Reputation is an intangible asset that is easy and expensive to lose. Building a company reputation mirrors building a personal reputation, but this can cause tension for CEOs between corporate reputation and their own. In situations of reputation risk and crisis, how you respond in the moment becomes how you are remembered. All the aspects of reputation building are vital for leaders from diverse backgrounds, because reputation promotes and protects.

Chapter 5

Understanding reputation

Reputation is tricky. It's highly valuable and easy to lose. It's deeply tied to what you say and how you say it, yet it's not completely within your control. It's complex and hard to measure, and bigger than the sum of its parts. And it's a way for us to address the glacial and anaemic change in the C-Suite.

Why reputation matters for diverse leaders

Your reputation is every part of landing, keeping or creating your dream leadership role. As we saw in previous chapters, all the interviewees are very thoughtful about how they behave and how they speak. They are highly aware of how they are perceived. In a post I wrote on LinkedIn recently about reputation, I said while not everyone wants to be an influencer, everyone wants to have a good reputation. A commentor responded that leaders need to act as leaders, rather than thinking about claims or perception. While acting as a leader rather than claiming to be one is indeed important, it's only leaders who look like the traditional leadership norm who have the privilege of not thinking about perception. People who experience bias at work and in their everyday lives are hyper-aware of perception.

Perception, as this chapter will show, is critical to building reputation – whether it's that of a company, a CEO or someone building their leadership career. How you are seen is just as important as what you say.

Reputation is money

Reputation scholar and author of the 1996 book *Reputation: Realizing Value from the Corporate Image*, Charles Fombrun, showed that reputation creates wealth. He was the first person to link the corporate image to value, or what he called intangible wealth or reputational capital.[1] Fombrun explained that companies 'have become the modern icons of our mass society. Not only do we dance to the tune of their decisions, but we increasingly worship at the high altar of their fame.'[2]

Since Fombrun's book came out, there have been massive changes in how we communicate. Social media means there is more focus on individuals rather than companies. CEOs are as much modern icons as the companies they work for.

But companies are still highly vulnerable to reputational risk. According to researchers Eccles, Schatz and Newquist: 'In an economy where 70% to 80% of market value comes from hard-to-assess intangible assets such as brand equity, intellectual capital, and goodwill, organizations are especially vulnerable to anything that damages their reputations.'[3]

Reputation is complex

Fombrun's definition of corporate reputation is: 'A perceptual representation of a company's past actions and future prospects that describes the firm's overall appeal to all of its key constituents when compared with other leading rivals.'[4]

One the things that this definition, written in 1996, lacks is the idea of the present. Given that Fombrun wrote his book before the advent of social media, at a time when communication was less instantaneous and available to all, this is understandable. Social media now gives reputation a sense of urgency – one mistake can be disseminated around the world in seconds, as we saw with the Kyte Baby scandal in Chapter 1. It's a short step from TikTok to CNN.

While Fombrun's definition is for companies, it contains many of the same elements of personal reputation: the perception of others, ways you have acted in the past, a sense of how you might act in the future, your general appeal, your audience and your competitors.

We live in a complex world, and we view entities through multiple lenses. Organizations can have different reputations with different people for different things. For example, a company can be loved by the non-governmental organizations that receive its corporate social responsibility grants, treated with suspicion by activists for not commenting on burning social justice issues, admired by financial analysts for demonstrating consistent growth, despised by employees because of recent layoffs, liked by its local community for donating to schools, adored by former employees who remember the good old days and ignored by potential talent for not being cutting-edge enough. All these perceptions are possible, all at the same time.

This means that a company's reputation is more than the sum of its parts, or an aggregate of many things. Polish academic Danuta Szwajca calls it 'multiaspect.'[5]

With multiple audiences (each of which can contain multiple perspectives), blurring of lines between internal and external brought on by social media, the proliferation of Internet sites where company and leadership behaviour can be adjudicated, this idea that reputation is more than the sum of its parts means that the view of all audiences is critical. And it makes it even harder to measure.

One of the things I always bemoaned as communicator is that there is no single simple way to define and track reputation, the way Net Promoter Score (NPS) measures customer loyalty and satisfaction. People have tried, but things got complicated.

Reputation is hard to measure

In 1999, Fombrun created the Reputation Institute with Rotterdam academic Cees von Riel. They partnered with Lou Harris, owner of market research company Harris Interactive, to create the Harris-Fombrun Corporate Reputation Quotient (CRQ) Model, which measures stakeholder perception.[6] It used six dimensions – emotional appeal, products and services, workplace environment, financial performance, vision and leadership, and social responsibility – broken down into 20 attributes, which poll respondents rank.

An adjusted version of the model continues to be used in The Harris Poll, which is now known as the Axios-Harris Poll 100 and is an annual ranking of the reputations of the top 100 most visible US companies. The poll now ranks companies according to trust, vision, growth, products and services, culture, ethics and citizenship.

In 2014, The Harris Poll was sold to Nielsen in 2014 and in 2017 to The Stagwell Group. Nielsen still owns the wordmark 'reputation quotient.'

When Harris and Fombrun parted ways, the Reputation Institute went on to create the RepTrak model to replace CRQ in 2005. In 2020, the institute changed its name to RepTrak and Fombrun remains founder and chairman emeritus. RepTrak measures the reputation of the top 100 global companies. The ranking is based on survey data from 234,000 respondents across 14 major economies and does not include corporate self-reporting. The dimensions measured are products and services (same as 1999), performance (same), leadership (same), innovation (new since the initial poll), conduct (new), workplace (same) and citizenship (new name but arguably the same meaning as social responsibility).

A third reputation measurement is the Fortune 500, which ranks US companies and in a separate poll global companies, by revenue only. However, Fortune does produce a list of most admired companies. Companies are ranked on nine dimensions – quality of leadership and management, quality of products and services, innovativeness, long-term investment value, financial soundness, talent attraction and retention, community responsibility, wise use of corporate assets, effectiveness in conducting a global business – by a network of 4,000 business insiders.

These complex multiple dimensions – the fact that reputation is multi-aspect – are what make it hard to measure.

All the reputation measurements focus on what people say about you. But what about what you say about yourself? How does that play a role in reputation?

Reputation goes two ways

Rupert Younger directs the Oxford University Centre for Corporate Reputation. In 2017 he co-authored *The Reputation Game*, with David Waller, a former *Financial Times* journalist. Its subtitle is 'The Art of Changing How People See You' and the gist of their argument is that reputation is a game and if you understand the rules, you can play it successfully. They say:

> 'Companies with top-flight reputations hire and retain the best people, charge more for their products, achieve better profit margins and benefit from higher share ratings, creating a virtuous cycle. Companies with poor reputations, on the other hand, have trouble hiring and keeping people, get treated with suspicion by government and regulators, and are shunned by customers and investors alike.'[7]

Waller and Younger say there are three parts to the reputation game: behaviours, networks and narratives. Behaviours send signals about who you are. Networks shape perceptions of who you are. How you use narratives influences how people see you.

Inherent in their story is the two-way function of reputation: you can control what you do, say and who you associate with (in order to influence your reputation as much as possible) but you can't control or manage how this lands with your audience. And as we saw above, you can have different reputations with different people for different things.

However, if you are aware of the rules of the game, as Waller and Younger define it, you can play it more successfully.

Porter Braswell, whom we met in Chapter 2, says that his ability to consistently deliver on his ideas is what has allowed him to build a strong reputation in the business world:

> 'Anything that I've built, anybody else could have built... But what I've been able to do consistently for the last decade is deliver what I said I was going to deliver. That led to a reputation or brand of delivering the highest quality possible... and that reputation gives the benefit of the doubt for all things that I work on. Without that, I'm just another voice in the orchestra of voices and fighting for attention.'

Porter's perspective is that his reputation is built on a cultivated track record of success and trustworthiness, However, as a Black man, his identity has been another crucial factor in shaping his business path. The odds are already daunting for founders, but they're triply stacked against Black founders who are not getting access to capital at nearly the same rates as their white counterparts, Porter explains.

'There's this constant sense of trying to have to prove yourself,' he says about his mindset as he built his first company. 'That was my first phase of leadership. And as a Black person, knowing the odds against me led to me fighting for the business to be successful.'

While navigating the difficulties that come with trying to build a business as a Black founder can be daunting, Porter believes that his difference and 'the lack of people who look like [him] doing the work… is actually a huge asset.' He stands out for his ability to speak from his unique lived experiences, which was useful in early rounds of capital where he could use his own experience to explain why diversity recruitment is important. 'I'm the expert educating somebody who is supposed to be an expert on everything about a thing they have no idea about… It's become a competitive advantage for me.'

Porter successfully navigated a business landscape that typically excludes people of colour by leveraging the strength of his lived experience and developing a stellar reputation over time, eventually enabling him to stand out in a crowded field as a thought leader, successfully sell Jopwell, and raise revenue for his current company, 2045 Studio.

Porter shows that his narrative has shifted. He built a reputation based on successfully having run and sold Jopwell. Now, combining that experience with speaking with authority about being a Black man in the US, he is in a position to educate investors. His book (*Let Them See You*), and his role as a thought leader, support this narrative. And, if you remember from Chapter 2, Porter changed his leadership behaviour to a more approachable style. His behaviour also speaks to his reputation.

Thinking back to Chapter 1 where we talked about context (crisis for leaders) and conduct (crisis of leaders), context is often the uncontrollable factor when it comes to reputation. Context usually shows up as a crisis, and how you behave before, during and after a crisis will affect reputation. However, if you've built a level of trust with your audiences before the crisis, they are more likely to trust you during it.

This is an idea I learned from the co-founder and chief strategy officer of Staffbase, Frank Wolf. He calls it the narrative moat.

Building your narrative moat

Frank's recent book, *The Narrative Age*, sets out the thesis that reputation consists of narratives, and narratives consist of stories. 'Narratives enable strategic control over the organization's reputation. While individual stories are important components of the way in which an organization is perceived, narratives offer a more consistent, coherent and practical approach to reputation management.'[8]

Think of Ernesto in Chapter 4: after arriving in a board role, he realized his team needed to be on the same page on certain critical HR topics. He invested time in creating white papers on those topics so that the team had a consistent set of stories. With that single source of truth, they were able to cohere around their key narratives and reputation as a team.

Frank says that a moat in the business context is a company's competitive advantage that is difficult for competitors to imitate or overcome, and a strong narrative moat – built from the inside out – also builds long-lasting competitive advantages.[9]

A narrative moat is not a one-time action. You build the moat, and hence your reputation, over time.

> 'Think of it as tending a garden; you can't just plant seeds and walk away, expecting them to grow. You need to water, nurture and protect them regularly. Similarly, a company's reputation isn't built overnight or with a single campaign. Just like any other competitive advantage, it requires consistent effort, care and attention.'[10]

How identity helps

We talked about how Porter's identity ties in with his reputation. Another leader who talks about the relationship between identity and reputation is Paul Nolan. Paul is co-owner and COO of CCGroup, a UK-based PR and marketing agency for the tech industry and has worked his entire career in PR. Paul received an adult ADHD diagnosis at the age of 42.

He said this brought him relief because understanding the condition better and having access to appropriate medication, meant he could be 'calmer for longer' and less erratic. As the co-owner of a business and a leader, Paul's hyperfocus has always been helpful when working on one thing at a time. Now he understands better why he struggles to juggle.

Paul does not suffer from stigma. 'I'm an open book; I wear my heart on my sleeve, and I can laugh at things, especially myself.' He believes being open about his diagnosis is the best thing to do:

'I think the only way we're really going to overcome the stigma that surrounds neurodiversity is to reveal how many people it affects. I can understand that some people don't feel the same level of comfort as me, but I think it's important that more people like me create this comfort by talking about their own experiences to legitimize them even more.'

He is very focused on building an inclusive culture at CCGroup, where employees can show up as their authentic selves, whether they are neurodiverse, neurotypical or have other identities. His diagnosis has helped him coach other leaders in how to manage their neurodiverse team members, and he realizes that the business needs to refocus on how they measure performance to allow neurodiverse colleagues to flourish.

Paul's identity is now part of how people perceive him – his reputation – and he is consciously building a culture where others can own their identities. He is building a culture based on trust.

Role of trust

Researchers and academics see trust as an important constituent of reputation. Fombrun states that 'the more trustworthy a company appears to its key constituents, the better regarded a company will be.'[11] In her book, *Who Can You Trust: How Technology Brought Us Together and Why It Might Drive Us Apart*, trust expert Rachel Botsman documents the loss of trust in institutions and a shift towards distributed trust (between individuals enabled by networks and platforms). In it she says that: 'Reputation is trust's closest sibling: the overall opinion of what people think of you. It's the opinion others have formed based on past experiences and built up over days, months, sometimes years. In that sense, reputation, good or bad, is a measure of trustworthiness.'[12]

Trust figures in the general public's trust in an organization, as filtered through its reputation, which is managed and mitigated via the person-to-person relationship between the CEO and the CCO.

John Blakey focuses on the trust habits of individual leaders. His nine habits of leadership trust are based on the model that trustworthiness = ability × integrity × benevolence. I see these as strongly mapping to reputation, in that character is reflected in integrity × benevolence and competence matches with ability.[13] And Rachel Botsman says the three key traits of trustworthiness are honesty, reliability and competence[14], which also map to the key reputational traits.

In other words, the qualities that underpin a good reputation are the same qualities that underpin your trustworthiness.

Conclusion

Reputation is two-way – what you say about yourself and how others experience you. What you say is the starting point and what you can control, which is why all the diverse leaders I interviewed are intentional about how they use language and how they show up. Your identity is part of how people perceive you and it can be powerful – however, you own your identity and how and when you want it to surface in the conversation.

Trust is reputation's closest sibling, and when you break trust (usually when your words don't match your behaviour), you damage your reputation.

From this chapter: Lessons in leadership communication

- Your reputation is every part of landing, keeping or creating your dream leadership role.
- Reputation is much more than the sum of its parts.
- The reputation game has three elements: narratives, behaviours and networks.
- Building a narrative moat is a competitive advantage and part of protecting your reputation in the long run.
- Reputation is built from the inside out.
- Reputation is a measure of trustworthiness.

Chapter 6

Understanding corporate versus CEO reputation

C EO and corporate reputation are deeply enmeshed. One affects the other, and can have massive cost implications for an organization. Two events that happened in the week of 12 September, 2023, provide a great example of this.

First, the then CEO of BP, Bernard Looney, announced that he was leaving the company after failing to disclose fully during an internal review the number of personal relationships he had been having with BP employees. This was variously described in news headlines as 'It's been mismanaged: Shocking exit of BP's CEO leaves the oil giant in a state of chaos,'[1] 'BP CEO Bernard Looney resigns after past relationships with colleagues'[2] and 'BP shares sink after CEO quits over relationships.'[3]

His behaviour, a failure of character, had a negative effect on the BP share price.

Second, the CEO of Citigroup, Jane Fraser, announced that she was removing five layers of management as part of a massive organizational overhaul. Headlines responded with 'Citigroup to strip out five layers of management under CEO Jane Fraser's revamp,'[4] 'Citigroup's business heads in revamped structure'[5] and 'Citigroup reorganizes under CEO Fraser. The stock is up.'[6]

Her behaviour – a restructuring smartly managed – caused the share price to rise. Hers was a triumph of competence.

These show how closely linked CEOs are to company reputation and company value, and it highlights two essential elements of reputation: character and competence. Waller and Younger say: 'You can have an outstanding capability reputation, while suffering an appalling character reputation. Sometimes your character reputation can be so bad it overwhelms your capabilities; at other times, your character flaws are forgiven because you are capable when it matters.'[7]

The ability to manage change successfully is one of many requirements in the CEO's skillset. While change management is often cast as an internal corporate process, failure can be very public. With the blurring of boundaries between internal and external, an employee knows what a financial analyst, a journalist, an activist or a member of the public knows. Jane Fraser's brutal pruning of five layers of management at Citigroup might have been received as a failed change if an employee had pre-emptively leaked it to a journalist. Credit to the Citigroup CCO for keeping it contained.

CEOs are under a raft of performance pressures. Managing their reputation, and that of the company, is only one of the things they have to do on a very long list. They operate in a dynamic where they must both preserve and change their organizations to match internal and external pressures. The need to execute and improve (stability) while competing to be fast and innovative (change) is a form of ambidexterity and a survival mechanism to prevent obsolescence.[8] And it is in this soup of flux and continuous change where CEOs and CCOs spend much of their time together working on strategies for reputation.

According to Ansell et al., 'Institutions use strategies of dynamic adaption to help preserve a long-term relation between the institution's internal constellation and its social environment.'[9] The writers state that adaption is either pre-emptive (reform before a threat becomes manifest) or reactive (damage control or crisis management). This is a useful way to frame how CEOs and CCOs consider reputation – something that they either build against possible threat or something they manage when threat is manifest.

Neither reputation management for organizations and CEOs nor relationship building between CEOs and CCOs happen in vacuums. Context is always present, especially in terms of reading the environment for reputational risk.

The elements of competence, character and context are critical to CEO and company reputation. In Chapter 1, we learned that CEOs are also expected to make sense of context for their audiences. We call this coherence – and this is where the CCO's role becomes really important.

How CEO reputation affects company reputation

It is very difficult to prise the CEO's reputation from company reputation. They are often enmeshed and intertwined. A new CEO might bring a fresh reputation to an old company, or their reputation can be subsumed into company reputation when business is bad. Waller and Younger call this the portability of reputations.[10]

This is something that's important for leaders from diverse backgrounds to bear in mind: you might be allergic to self-promotion or putting yourself out there, but the portability of your reputation might help to land you the next great leadership role or build your dream company.

Portability

Tony Jamous incorporated a new company called Oyster shortly before the pandemic. Oyster is a global employment solution that helps companies hire all over the globe with all compliance and local payroll complexities covered. Having successfully exited his previous company after selling it to Ericcson for $6.5 billion at the age of 35,

Tony did not ever need to work again. Despite his manifested wealth and success, he says he was miserable.

He started Oyster based on the conviction that employees all over the world deserve fair and equitable opportunities no matter where they live. This was based on his childhood experience of observing the war in Lebanon first hand, and later fleeing to France with his family as a refugee.

'When I started this business in January 2020, we had no brand, and the pandemic happened.' Two years after its launch Oyster was valued at over $1 billion, making it a unicorn. At the time of writing four years later, it had just received Series D funding – which is the stage at which established start ups secure more investment to expand even further.

Tony has built a following of more than 80,000 people on LinkedIn, where he talks about running a business that is 100% remote and about his mission of conscious leadership. As someone who'd been CEO of a different company, Tony realized he had a brand that was portable that would be of benefit to the business. 'I thought, why don't I put myself out there, and it worked. People wanted to hear from me about remote work and it became a driver of leads for the business. It became a customer acquisition strategy.'

One of the interviewees who has been a CEO of several highly successful companies has a unique perspective on the portability of reputation. Michele Bettencourt is the chairperson of a large NASDAQ company, executive chair of another company and sits on several boards. In her Silicon Valley career, Michele has been CEO of four other companies, many of which she led to successful buyouts.

Michele was born Anthony Bettencourt (who she refers to as AB) in Fremont, California, to a family she describes as 'not privileged, by any means.' Her father was a blue-collar labourer, and her mother stayed at home to raise the family. Michele's dream as a child was to become a tech writer and earn $40,000 a year, which would make her rich beyond dreams in comparison to her father's salary of $17,000 a year. However, a talent for sales projected her into senior roles and by the age of 34 was VP of sales for a large company. At 45, she won the Ernst and Young Entrepreneur of the Year Award. She says, 'I've opened the NASDAQ twice as CEO, twice as a board member. I've opened the NYSE once as CEO, done all the things one probably wants to do in a career.'

At the same time as all this success, there was another narrative happening. 'I've always felt different. I don't know what it was. I didn't roam around saying I'm in the wrong body. That wasn't it. But this other thing was going on with me. I couldn't quite figure it out, and it every time it would get out of control, I'd dress up and go out at night on trips for work, and then I'd throw everything away.'

After her father died in 2016, Michele says she 'was a mess.' She left her home and family in California, moved to New York and began transitioning. She returned for a holiday in 2019, Covid struck, and she stayed. Michele still lives with her wife and has great relationships with her three daughters.

After her transition, she was approached for CEO roles. However, she decided to focus on board roles where she could still provide her expertise. Michele says she communicates differently now: 'I was always fearful of hurting people's feelings as AB. I didn't like confrontation. No one does, but I really hated it. I wasn't as clear a communicator as I thought I was. Now, I tend to be much better at listening, at just having an opinion, at saying what I mean.'

Michele says her wife believes that this is as much to do with age as with transitioning. She also says people do treat her differently as Michele. 'I think there are occasions where people will talk over me. I'm chair of the board, so they shouldn't do that.' However, the biggest change for her is employees reaching out to get her advice about transitioning. She has become a resource for people who are dealing with it themselves or in their families.

Some research has shown that CEOs can build their reputation in tandem with other allies. Boivie, Graffin and Gentry looked at the role of financial analysts in shaping CEO reputation, while Love et al., researched three factors that they assumed play into CEO's ability to gain prominence for their firms: media attention, industry awards and whether they are 'outsider CEOs' (who tend to be portrayed as corporate saviours).[11] They found the first two to be significant, but the third not.

How CEOs talk about reputation

The CEOs I interviewed say that CEO and company reputation are both equally important, and they're clear on the mix between company and their own reputation. According to Sean, the US-based CEO of a global tech company:

> 'My personal brand, if it's positive, has some modest impact on the company that I'm leading. If my personal brand is negative, it has massive impact on the company I am leading. So I think your personal brand has to be at worst neutral, to slightly positive. If you're going to be a CEO, I don't think that you can be an effective CEO in the world we live in if your personal brand is negative.'

He says he uses social media extensively to build his reputation:

> 'I'll say that I spend a disproportionately high amount of time on reputation building. I am very present on social. I tend to lean more towards business oriented social so LinkedIn and Twitter and my Twitter is primarily used for business related reasons. And interestingly, I do it more frequently my third time as CEO than I did even my first time as CEO. I'd say four to six hours per week of dedicated reputation building time.'

He acknowledged that meeting press, analysts, customers and partners also played a part in building his reputation, but he clearly delineated time on social media as an important part of building and maintaining his reputation.

A female CEO of a tech company in India said that CEO and company reputation go:

> 'hand in hand... but at the same time, there is also a strong need to establish yourself as a leader in the tech space given that we are also working with the governments, with industry bodies, with academia... also as a leader, being credible being known for what I stand for in technology.'

Mike Ettling, CEO of Unit 4 – a global enterprise software company – says his philosophy on this is 'very much that you build the reputation for the company and your reputation as a CEO derives from that... I've never sat down with a comms person and said, right, are you going to go and build my brand.'

He describes how he intersperses company thought leadership with personal reflections on his social media.

Aspirin and vitamins

Sean uses a great metaphor:

> 'I always think about reputation building in the context of aspirin and vitamins. I think most people that spend all their time taking aspirins are in a reactive state. And humans generally, if you're clear about who your company is, what you believe in, what you stand for, what you care about, and you're focused on customers and partners, but I believe even more importantly, you're focused on employees and your reputation building. Those are vitamins and they generally prevent headaches.'

It's interesting that all CEOs I spoke to used the word 'brand' when I asked them about reputation. And while brand and reputation are often conflated, and can even sit in the same corporate communications departments, I'm actively choosing to use the language around reputation rather than the language around brand, branding or personal brands. The difference for me is summarized in Waller and Younger's definition that you can pay for a brand, but you cannot buy a reputation.[12]

However, the use of brand to describe personal reputation points to something that has completely changed how CEOs communicate – social media. And while some of my readers might be highly digitally savvy and can't imagine a world without it, some readers will remember a time before. Many of the CEOs I interviewed have had to navigate the shift. Some have done so brilliantly, while some struggle and others still try to pretend it doesn't exist.

Social media has brought about a seismic shift in reputation.

The role of social media

Before social, corporate boundaries were thick and impenetrable. CEOs could say and behave one way behind the wall, and say and behave another way on the outside. They had complete control over messages to their audiences, whether internal or external. Leaks could occur, but since newspapers were published locally, a leak in Germany wouldn't make the news in the US and vice versa. Even if it eventually did, timing was slow and would allow for leeway to neutralize the story.

In the years between the launch of the first chatroom in 1973, LinkedIn in 2003, Facebook in 2004, YouTube in 2005, Twitter (now X) in 2006[13] and now, those boundaries have effectively dissolved. Leaked information can and does go viral, is immediate, global, and anonymity protects the leaker. Corporate is now porous, and CEOs have a much harder time controlling messaging. Behaviour also no longer hides behind corporate walls – with anonymous employee review sites like Glassdoor and Indeed, the world knows how CEOs show up.

I was hired into my first executive communications role in 2012 with the express directive to help executives navigate social media. I had been a stay-at-home parent for the past ten years, had written a novel while my children were in *Kindergarten* and blogged the process. I had developed a level of comfort with Wordpress, Facebook and Twitter/X that made me a viable candidate the same way new communications hires have TikTok expertise today. The first executive I worked with had zero interest in social media; he was not persuadable. However, the second executive was, and I got him started on Twitter – very scripted (by me) and stilted, but a start.

Social media management has become a key part of every executive's reputation toolbox. And it's key to proactively managing reputation – Frank Wolf's narrative moat. The stories executives tell about themselves, their companies, their strategies, their interests lay down an ever-widening moat that protects and buffers them against the bad times.

The role of proactive reputation management was key to all my thesis interviewees.

Proactive reputation management

Abigail, a very senior head of marketing and communications, said that as a leadership team they spend 'a lot of time on proactive reputation building simply because the last two years we were in the process of selling the company. ..to make sure that the view was very positive, and we were perceived as a high value company.'

Most respondents said they spend more time on proactive activities. I asked them to put a proportion on it, and their estimates ranged from 90:10 proactive to reactive to 60:40. A CCO called Liam said in his current company it is 85:15 but that he had worked at other companies where this was flipped towards reactive activities, while another agreed that it can easily swing the other way if there is an issue or a crisis.

Of the two who did not say they spent more time working proactively on reputation, one was managing a crisis at the time of the interview and the other works for a company that is in a long-term process of reputational repair.

Stakeholder management

Within these proactive activities, CEOs and CCOs work intensively and consciously on stakeholder management. Most CCOs shape their communications departments into audience management teams (internal communications for employees, PR for the media, social media for the public, analyst relations for the analyst community, investor relations for the financial analysts, public affairs for government relations – depending on the size and function of the company).

Liam has a reputation risk team, which he described as 'small but beautifully formed... who do nothing but spend their time considering short-term, medium-term and long-term reputational risks to the business.' Amanda, who is head of marketing and communications, talked about, how on arriving in her current business, she found the lack of analyst relations to be a reputational threat and focused on building up the function immediately. Prenessa, a CCO, told me how she actively uses LinkedIn as a means of communication with the board, as another stakeholder group. This is something I see often – executives using LinkedIn as a way to show internal audiences (in other words, their bosses) what a great job they are doing.

CEOs and CCOs also plan how to communicate to different audiences and how to manage the messages. A CEO told me that while the messages are similar, they also 'tailor' them accordingly. Planning messaging can take place months in advance.

One head of communication described how, know that a reduction in force (RIF) was on the horizon, they began preparing the narrative and using related language six months in advance. Mike Ettling explained a similar activity around RIF, in which even though the outcome was ultimately negative, in that people were laid off, they had focused on a telling a story so that those who remained in the company were able to understand and repeat it. He calls this 'the barbeque test' which for him means that CEOs and CCOs should provide a story so clear and simple that employees can repeat it to their friends at a barbeque. This is one way of getting ahead of the rumour mill, which can threaten reputation. Sometimes messaging does not land well: the CCO I interviewed who was in the middle of a crisis described how her well-planned brand relaunch was being scuppered by a handful of disgruntled ex-employees saying negative things about the company online.

In proactive reputation management, there's a lot of talk about messaging. It may sound creepy and a bit like spin, but what it really is is sense-making. It's about explaining why things matter and creating meaning. The idea of creating meaning came up consistently in the interviews with diverse leaders, and for them it comes down to the use of language. Words, as the way to deliver meaning and build connections, really matter.

Why proactive reputation management matters for diverse leaders

Building a narrative moat and being proactive about reputation is important for all leaders but it is especially important for diverse leaders who need to be visible for several reasons.

Gone are the days when it was enough to do your job and do it well. You also need to be seen doing it well. Your surface area of luck (or your chance of being lucky) is your activity (passionate doing) multiplied by the number of people you effectively communicate your passion and activities to (effective telling).[14]

Stanford University professor, Jeffrey Pfeffer, says perception can change the negotiating dynamic during an interview process: 'Instead of competing for a job and selling yourself to the board and senior executives, if you have a stellar reputation, companies will be fighting to hire you.'[15]

Most of the of this book is about effective telling, how leaders do it and how you can, but it's important to consider why.

Representation matters

Vuyi from Chapter 4 mentioned how taken aback she was at the emotional reaction she received in her organization when she became one of the most senior and visible Black leaders in the company. She realized that representation matters, and her promotion showed others that it was possible to rise in that organization. You are a role model to those coming after you.

This is not without friction for some. A couple of leaders who I asked to be part of the interview cohort said they were uncomfortable being called out as a female leader, and chose not to be interviewed. They just wanted to be a leader, known for the success of their business not their gender.

This a delicate balance I used to tread when I was doing executive communications for women in senior leadership positions. We ensured we balanced out the number of engagements they did between business topics, such as innovation and digital transformation, with engagements on women in leadership. They knew both were important, but wanted to avoid always being seen to be speaking on 'the women topic.'

Maya Dadoo is a female leader who did agree to be interviewed. She is CEO and co-founder of Worky, a Mexico HR and payroll start-up, and only one of three female Series A tech CEOs in Mexico. (Series A is the next level of funding a startup receives after seed funding.) Maya identifies as Latin American with Indian heritage and an engineer. She told me that having been previously resistant to being seen as 'the female CEO,' she now recognizes that representation is important and wants to connect more with other women who run tech or SaaS companies in Mexico.

Kholi told me about turning up to a client with an all-women team. As a country that has transitioned from apartheid to democracy, South Africa has had very specific legal requirements for companies to transform their own demographics. It's less about representation than it is about transformation. 'How visible we are in driving diversity and inclusion becomes very critical, not only from a compliance perspective, but also it becomes visible to the market.' She told me that customers had commended her on the company's transformation when she arrived for a meeting with a team of women.

Having a voice

And it's more than representing, it's about giving yourself permission to have a platform, to be seen and heard. Vania de Stefani is the CEO of an industry cooperative response management organization that serves the oil and gas industry. She identifies as a female CEO who is a single parent. Born in Italy, she has worked in several countries and now lives in the UK.

Vania is diverse in several ways: she is a female leader in a male-dominated industry, an Italian in the UK, and although she now holds a PhD in thermphysics, she originally trained and worked as a classical flautist. Vania says her voice is very important to her. 'I always want to be heard, be visible and have a platform.' Her trademark is that she always wears red shoes, because 'I always want to make a mark.'

Conclusion

In this chapter, we've seen that CEOs focus on proactive reputation management more than reactive reputation mitigation. This means creating a narrative moat, or a protective competitive advantage that shows how you differentiate from others. CEOs talk about personal brand and reputation interchangeably, but to them, this means having an active presence on social media. CEOs' and senior leaders' reputations are portable, which means they can be taken from one job to another. Your reputation foreshadows your next job.

What happens when companies and leaders neglect proactive reputation management? Risk is everywhere and crises are unpredictable. There is no knowing when one will hit. We'll take a look at this in the next chapter.

From this chapter: Lessons in leadership communication

- Your reputation is portable – it might get you to the next great job.
- Your achievements are always your achievements – make sure you talk about them.
- Those following you, and who see you as a role model, want to see you shine.
- If you stand out, like Vania, own it.
- Social media is part of every leader's reputation toolbox.

Chapter 7

Reputational risk and crisis management

Reputational risk is the possibility of crisis. Crisis is an active situation of threat. I deal with them together because they are closely knit, but crisis is often characterized by emergency and lack of time (which can lead to bad decisions that later need to be rescinded), while reputational risk requires constant management.

What the academics say

We've seen that reputation can be complex.

For Danuta Szwajca, it's this complexity that leads to challenges in corporate reputation risk management.[1] She says the friction comes when management try to undertake a linear approach to risk management (plan, implement, control) while reputational risk is multi-disciplinary and systemic. She says that reputational risk is the 'risk of risks.' This means its source is usually some other kind of risk, whether its social, financial, operational or behavioural. Risk of risks speaks to the human element, since reputational risk or crises usually occur thanks to the people's behaviour (think of Bernard Looney, former CEO of BP).

The pressure of time is usually one of the biggest factors, and a reputation built over years 'can be devastated in a remarkably short time.'[2]

In their much-cited 2007 *Harvard Business Review* article, Eccles, Newquist and Schatz say that most companies do a poor job of handling their reputations and risks to them. 'They tend to focus their energies on handling the threats to their reputations that have already surfaced. This is not risk management; it is crisis management – a reactive approach whose purpose is to limit the damage.'[3]

According to Eccles and his co-researchers, three things determine which companies are vulnerable to reputational risk: (1) exceeding their character (they call this the reputation-reality gap); (2) when external beliefs and expectations of the company change; and (3) weak internal coordination.

Some responses to crises might include what another group of researchers, Mitnick, Mahon and McGowan, call 'privatizing.'[4] This is the process of bringing the crisis inhouse and trying to limit external commentary. An example that comes to mind in the UK is the infamous Partygate scandal in Boris Johnson's prime ministership, during which he spent many weeks refusing to comment as it was being investigated internally by Sue Gray.[5] This went on for so long and to such an extent that her name was associated with several memes.[6]

They also suggest redefining subsequent crises so that they appear different from earlier ones, shifting the focus from the crisis to the repair. Johnson provides a rich seam of examples: to deflect from the failures of NHS funding he would point to the fantasy of '40 new hospitals.'[7]

A final suggestion from the authors is to redefine corporate identity so that the old achievement sets no longer apply, and they provide the example of Phillip Morris renaming itself Altria in 2003. Altria means 'high' and was seen as an attempt to create a positive resonance around the tobacco industry (though in 2019, they split again). The authors say that many of these actions around crisis are ethically questionable and can lead to a loss of trust.

Capability and character dynamics become highly visible in a crisis. 'Capability reputations are extremely sticky, while character reputations are much more volatile.'[8]

Companies aim to manage reputation competently before it crystallizes into a crisis, so much so that the academic literature urges the need to create a Chief Reputation Officer.[9] I remember reading this and thinking, 'Well, that's the chief communications officer.' But then I found that the CCO was almost completely missing from academic literature.

Boolean searches in the Business Search Ultimate and ABI Inform databases for 'chief communications officer' or 'head of communications' with CEO and either relationship or reputation revealed little. When I did a simple search on 'chief communications officer' or 'head of communications,' the articles were on hiring or firing of CCOs. Searches that removed the CCO/head of communications and positioned the CEO in relationship to communications and reputation provided further articles, none of which mention the head of communications in helping the CEO or the company improve their reputation. The active role of the head of communications in managing these (either alone or in tandem with the CEO) is invisible. The CCO was the missing actor in the reputation play, which was why I decided to dig deeper by interviewing several pairs.

How the CEO and CCO work together on reputational risk and crisis management

When talking about risk, CEOs and COOs speak either about those that are common across industries (cyber security, bad actors, bad behaviour) or risks that are specific to them. One CCO told me that in his industry, 'risk looks like the wallpaper.' A tech CEO said that 'change is risk,' while another tech CEO describes the three main risks he sees as disruptive technologies, data security and the war for talent. A fintech CEO talked eloquently about risk in terms of 'externalities', which he described as strategic, operational, market, liquidity, credit, customer, and 'internalities' such as fraud, corruption, cyber, bad actors. This echoes Szwajca's idea of risk of risks, and underlines how aware CEOs and CCOs of risk.

In response to the possibility of risk crystallizing into crisis, nearly all of the CEOs and CCOs I spoke to have clear crisis management protocols (or plans for when different types of crisis hit) in place. They role-play crisis situations and review their protocols frequently. Communications nearly always sits on the crisis management team, and most of the communicators I interviewed have crisis communications plans mapped to different reputational risk scenarios. One had as many as 40 different scenarios planned out.

We talked in the last chapter about proactive reputation management versus reactive, and the respondents (CEOs and CCOs) told me that 90% of their joint work was proactive. They focus on reputation building as a current pre-emptive measure against future volatility. One CCO talked about ex-employees attacking the business during a rebranding exercise and spoke of her struggles with damage control, since the CEO refused to be the face of the business and speak up during the crisis.

And know this: if you already have a good reputation in the market, and you have built a narrative moat of stories over the years, this will be ballast when the storm of crisis arrives. This explains why 90% of the interviewees focus on proactive reputation management: they know instinctively that proactive reputation building will mean that audiences are prepared to consider the company as a good actor with good intentions when crisis hits.

Case study: The layoffs in tech

We saw in Chapter 2 how some of the corporate DEI teams have been affected by the spate of layoffs since 2022. It's not just DEI. At the time of writing in 2024, 536 tech companies had laid off 149,690 employees. This came on top of 264,220 affected employees in 2023 and 165,269 in 2022.[10] Whether justified or not, layoffs have an effect on the humans involved, those who are retrenched, those who retrench and those who are not retrenched[11] – and women are the hardest hit.[12]

According to Forbes, 'The handling of these layoffs has sparked significant criticism. In many cases, companies have left employees in the dark for weeks or even months, fostering a toxic atmosphere of fear and uncertainty. It's a stark reminder that, despite claims that employees are their greatest asset, companies often sacrifice their workforce first in times of crisis—even when posting record profits. For example, Microsoft laid off 1,900 workers just five days before reporting a 17.6% increase in revenue to $62 billion, while Amazon dismissed a thousand workers despite a 14% rise in revenue to $170 billion. To make matters worse, some companies are rumored to be reducing severance packages right before layoffs, further eroding trust.'[13]

While layoffs tend to lead to share price increases, though not always,[14] there is a wider reputational issue at hand. Investors are not the only audiences. The retrenched employees will hold an opinion on how well or badly they have been treated, and they will definitely share those opinions with others. The company's reputation for handling a layoff well or badly will be affected by the employees who remain in the company, the media, customers and partners, and society at large.

X is renowned for a disastrous mass firing of 80% of its workforce in 2023.[15] Its value is now estimated to be 71% lower than when Musk bought it for $44 billion in 2022.[16] Where X stands today reputationally is a clear example of risk of risks – its reputation is tied to the owner's reputation (behavioural), the fact that he now allows hate speech and fake news free rein on the site (operational), and advertisers pulling out (financial).

In comparison, there are other tech companies that managed the layoffs well. They were considerate to their employees, offered decent severance packages, communicated humanely and well in advance – and made sure that their layoff communication was published publicly for all their audiences to read. Common factors in the layoff communications included: an apology with humane language, an explanation of why the decision was made, clarity on the guiding principles that led to the decision, who was affected and why, and very clear steps on what would happen next – both for the affected employees and those who remained.

For founders, layoffs might come when investors advise it. Worky CEO and founder Maya Dadoo told me that during the process of finding the next stage of funding, she had to reduce costs and lay off nearly 50% of her staff. She worked very hard at making sure the conversations with those affected were both kind and humane, and that each retrenched person received the full severance package according to Mexican law and support in finding a new job. However, from a communications point of view, she feels she neglected the remaining employees, and it took several weeks to get the organizational culture back on track and everyone working in the same direction.

I looked at 40 layoff letters that were published in the last three years. Here are some examples from those letters of humane language:

- 'I am deeply sorry to be taking this step... I thank you from the bottom of my heart... The work you did here matters and you will always be a part of the Hubspot story.' Hubspot CEO Yamini Rangan[17]

- 'I understand that this announcement may trigger strong emotions for all of you, whether your role is being impacted or not. All emotions are perfectly understandable and acceptable. Personally, I feel tremendous sadness that these decisions may unexpectedly impact the lives of Oyster teammates whom we care for deeply.' Oyster CEO Tony Jamous[18]
- 'We've written 134 Founder blogs since 2011, but this one comes with the heaviest of hearts knowing we are saying goodbye to great teammates and friends. We came to this decision as an executive team and with our board, but ultimately the final call is on us as co-founders. To those who are leaving us: we are deeply sorry.' Atlassian co-founders Mike Cannon-Brookes and Scott Farquhar[19]

What to do in an external reputational crisis

The most important thing to do in a reputational crisis is to minimize risk. This is hardest to do when emotions are high. For leaders and communicators, here's a handy list of things to remember.

Don't panic

The natural human response is raised cortisol, but the most important thing to remember is to control your emotions. One of my CCO interviewees described her personality as 'exuberant,' but in reputational risk situations her modus operandi is 'calm, calm, calm, calm.' Another said he makes sure not to: 'spook the herd. You know, it's one thing to know when to flag issues. But you should be the last person who panics or induces panic, because after a while, people will get tired of you always shouting.'

One interviewee said the worst thing in a crisis situation is panic: 'Ultimately, it's the most destructive emotion in the world, isn't it? You don't think straight... it clouds your judgement. You just don't hear what you need to hear.' You learn who to trust in crisis: 'It'd be like, yeah, next time, we're not going to involve that person because they just had a meltdown.'

The first thing you say is the most important thing

The next step is to carefully consider and measure your first public words. Whatever you say in the early hours of a crisis will be remembered and held against you (especially by the press) for eternity. Don't come out bullish and fighting; rather be measured and modest. The more senior your crisis spokesperson is the better. This will show the public how important it is to your company.

I was part of the crisis communications team when the company I was working for was accused of corruption in one of our locations. The local CEO made a bullish and (we later discovered) false first statement. Though we handled the crisis as well as possible in the days and weeks that followed, the press never let us forget those first words. They became the lens through which everything the company said and did was filtered.

Apologize

The common factor in all 40 of the good layoff letters I looked at is a sincere apology. If you're the leader, you have to own it. Even in the early hours of a crisis when you might not be sure what happened or what the details are, you still need to be human and apologize.

During the crisis I mentioned, our crisis team was divided on how to respond. Some felt that an apology would be bad for the brand. Others thought the company should say nothing. Eventually after several rounds of discussion, the executive leading the team agreed to acknowledge public sentiment and apologize. This significantly softened the media and the public's response both immediately and in the weeks that followed.

Be as transparent as you can be, but don't say everything

In the early hours of a crisis, you don't know everything. Instead of verbalizing assumptions about what happened (which could turn out to be wrong), be transparent about the steps that you will take.

Make reparations

If your company has done something actively bad, communicate how you plan to put this right. State when and how you will be providing updates on how you will resolve the crisis.

For leaders: trust your advisors

When our team was divided on how to respond, the people who wanted to protect the brand by saying nothing were the sales leaders. The people who knew the company had to make a statement that included an apology were the communication leaders. You don't ask communicators to make decisions about sales. Don't ask salespeople to make decisions about communications. Leaders, trust your communicators. They are there for a reason.

Having an internal communicator or communications consultant will help you manage a crisis in a humane and empathetic way – and help you to remember all your audiences to avoid reputational risk.

What to do in an internal crisis?

Internal crises fall into two categories: a reputational crisis that threatens to go external and a slow-burn change of culture. Layoffs fit into the former, but how do leaders manage the latter?

Kate is a VP at a tech company. When we spoke, the organization was in a high state of internal change and transformation that would affect how they operate in their industry. She explains the personal challenge of having to motivate and inspire: 'When the team goes through massive change and transformation, you as a leader need to motivate them, inspire them and give them a sense of direction. Finding that motivation within you to be able to inspire others, that for me, has been the biggest challenge.'

She says she has to show up for her team. Kate says in this situation her strategy is 'to tell the story in my own words, as authentically as possible.'

Kate explained to me how her leadership style has shifted towards authenticity over the years:

'I try to be myself now, because I learned the hard way. For the first ten years of my career, I was inspired by someone who was incredibly professional. She would never show emotion. And I thought I liked her attitude; I wanted to emulate that. I never allowed myself to be myself. I was always very professional, and I was also very knowledgeable. After 12 years in my role, I think it became very intimidating to the people who worked with me, I always had the answer to the questions. I appeared to be very confident.'

Her manager at the time encouraged her to ask her peers for feedback, and she was shocked to hear words like 'intimidating' and 'dominating.'

'It just broke my heart because I was exactly the opposite. I was insecure. I was not sure of myself. I would hide it in overconfidence. I said if this is the price for trying to be confident and professional then I will just be myself. Ever since then, I tell my team, I feel vulnerable right not, or I'm feeling good about this now.'

Kate says this change in her leadership communications style has served her well, and she now consistently gets high leadership trust scores from her team.

Learn from vulnerability

In times of internal crisis, it helps when leaders are vulnerable. Maya admits her tendency to present as perfect with all the answers makes it harder for people to help her – she is now trying to lean more on her board members and investors for help. She told me about a vulnerability exercise run by one of her investors for their start-up investees, in which she learned that male founders are under the same pressure and experience the same loneliness as female founders. 'The pressures are not unique to me or to female founders, and that was helpful for me to realize,' she says.

Liz Gebhard is a leader who has held several roles in large e-commerce businesses, her most recent being Head of Global Strategy and Operations for Employee Experience, Inclusive Experiences and Technology at Amazon. She described two challenges she experienced when she moved from the US to the UK to take on a global leadership role.

In the first one, Liz realized that while she was leading the collective team well, at times she was failing to meet the needs of individuals:

> 'I thought I'd created space for people to come to me if they needed to push back or challenge, but I did not factor in that openly challenging your leader is a behaviour rooted in Western business culture. For my employees in India or China, there was not an inherent safe space or culture to challenge or speak back to your leaders. It required more one to one care and discussions to uncover issues or feedback that you won't find out about until you dig quite deeply. I

was in a position where I was also supposed to be helping other global leaders build better team cultures, but I needed to model that first in my own team. It forced me to really think about style, the importance of learning about unique differences of teams and cultures, and how I approached everything.'

The second was when she had to take on leading a large commercial team fully remote during Covid across nine countries:

'It was quite a young workforce and the largest team I'd led at that scale up to that point. For most of them, it was their first job out of university or first role as people leader, so their entire experience was in this really unsettling time. Coupled with the challenges of building a high-performing but collaborative team culture, the business was on fire and growing in some places but also slowing down in others. My challenge as a leader was: How do you help your teams stay informed enough to know what's coming, but not overburden them so they can continue to deliver what's most critical?'

Liz says this situation was not something she could rely on data for or defaulting to the ways that she had been successful in the past. Coming from a high-performance culture to this meant she 'had to be really vulnerable, I had to be super open to making mistakes and being completely wrong, while focusing the team on moving quickly to solutions, and I was really uncomfortable for a while in that space.'

She learned that vulnerability is a good accelerator to learn faster, because she now knows to take a step back to figure out the 'why' before she jumps into solution mode. And she has learned to acknowledge this in the moment: 'Now I'm more comfortable saying, actually, I don't know that. Let me go back to you. You do not have to have it all together all the time and it's important for teams to see that behaviour modelled by leadership.'

A leader's preparedness to show their vulnerability helps with team cohesion. It means that others can feel safe and gain a sense that they belong. Brené Brown says: 'If leaders really want people to show up, speak out, take chances, and innovate, we have to create cultures where people feel safe – where their belonging is not threatened by speaking up.'[20]

And this is not just about being warm, fuzzy and conflict-avoidant: it is about opening space for the right kinds of conversations to happen that are key to innovation. Harvard Business School professor Linda Hill calls this 'creative abrasion.' She says you do not get innovation without diversity and conflict. 'Fundamentally, as a leader, if you want to get innovation, you need to amplify the differences in your organization, not minimize them.'[21]

What leaders of diverse identities can learn from risk and crisis

The key to all risk and crisis is being prepared. If you're a CEO with a diverse background, all eyes are on you, but you are not alone. Remember to partner with your CCO and invest time in making them your reputation manager – long before crisis hits. The work you will do together in preparation proactively builds reputation as ballast against a future crisis. It takes time but it's worth the investment.

When you face an internal culture challenge, trust yourself to be both authentically strong and authentically vulnerable. One does not cancel out the other. When you come out from behind the shell of perfection, you learn (Liz), connect (Kate) and get help (Maya). Vulnerability builds trust and trust builds reputation.

Conclusion

The vulnerability that Kate, Liz and Maya speak of is part of being human. They have all learned it is no longer necessary to present as perfect at work. Meg talked about being a leader in all her 'messiness' in Chapter 4. Diverse leaders are showing us the way. In the same way, a company that has been messy and acknowledges it is at fault is admitting to vulnerability, humanity and mistakes. Think of the humanity in the layoff letters from Hubspot, Oyster and Atlassian – how you show up in crisis shows others how you will treat them when the next crisis hits.

From this chapter: Lessons in leadership communication

- Reputational risk is the risk of risks.
- Build a proactive narrative moat now as insurance against future crisis.
- Have crisis protocols in place and when crisis hits (and it will) do not panic.
- In crisis, listen to your communicators. They know what to do, when and in what order. Give them the trust they deserve.
- In leadership, vulnerability is strength. People are more likely to follow you when you are authentic about how you feel.
- Your vulnerability, where appropriate, helps others feel safe – this encourages the diversity of opinion needed for real innovation.
- Vulnerability is an accelerator for learning – about yourself, your team and your business.

Chapter 8

Building a relationship to manage reputation

W e've seen how the reputation of the CEO and the reputation of the company are intertwined, and that what the CEO says and does can affect the share price. In a sense, the CEO is the reputation carrier for the business. In order to do this successfully, on top of all the other mission-critical parts of running a business – manage product, balance books, create and deliver on strategy, achieves sales figures, create a sales funnel, hire, attract and reward talent – the CEO needs a reputation manager. This is someone who thinks about the reputation of the company, and the reputation of the CEO, at all times.

And that is the chief communications officer.

Reputations are highly valuable, intangible and easy to lose. CEOs need to work with a reputation manager on both company and their own reputations. CEOs might claim that company reputation supersedes their own – but almost all the CEOs I spoke to in the course of my research have their own dedicated executive communications function or work on reputation with their CCO. And as we saw with Looney and Fraser in Chapter 6, CEO reputation can have an immediate financial effect on the company's share price.

Reputation is the context of every single CEO/CCO interaction. It is the soup in which they swim. Unlike the relationships with the CFO, CHRO, the CRO, the CTO, the CEO and the CCO cannot bond over numbers. This often makes those CEOs who've come up in the comfortable binary world of figures in spreadsheets uncomfortable.

One of the early interviewees was Liam, a head of communications at a FTSE 50 company, who told me that the CCO is the only executive who has the privilege of being able to speak truth to power in a way that other executives are not able.

I asked him for more clarity on this. Why does the CCO have the privilege to speak truth to power more than any other executive? He explained in an email:

> 'I think it's partly a function of the relationship of trust between the CCO and CEO, and partly that there is *unlikely to be an ulterior motive for the advice proffered, other than to protect the firm/principal from harm* – because that is your core job (unlike other Execs who have other priorities, e.g. the success of their own part of the business).' (My italics.)

Why does this matter for leaders from diverse backgrounds?

The glass ceiling is a metaphor for the idea that leaders from diverse backgrounds struggle to make it to the top jobs. They are also beset by the glass cliff and the challenge of shorter tenures. Researchers have shown that women (and I extrapolate this to mean leaders from all under-represented minorities (URM)) have more chance of making it through the glass ceiling when an organization is in crisis. The study by Michelle Ryan and Alexander Haslam of the University of Exeter shows that women are over-represented in precarious leadership positions.[1]

In addition to this, the tenure of female CEOs at Fortune 500 companies is on average three years shorter than that of men's – this was backed up by research from Russell Reynolds and Associates, which looked at 3,000 companies across 12 stock exchanges.[2] 'Several studies have shown that women and individuals from minority groups are too often into leadership roles when a company is in decline, stacking the odds against them before they start the job.'[3]

If candidates from URM struggle to get into the top jobs, only get these during times of crisis and then do not last longer in the roles, this underlines the fact that their reputation management is vital. They need to work on their reputations to land and keep those CEO roles, and, if and when things don't work out, take their portable reputations to the next job.

One of the interviewees was a local MD of a global business. She returned to the region after 18 long years. As a part of her thought leadership strategy, she picked an executive communicator and created the conditions for trust to grow. In that safe space, they built a strategy to develop the executive's presence over time. They revisit the strategy quarterly to see if they are making progress. There is deep respect in the relationship, but also the space to give honest feedback, have wild ideas, experiment and to say no.

She is now highly recognized and known in her location, has won several leadership awards and sits on prominent boards. As a pair, the CEO and her executive communicator have crafted an identity that is portable and which will carry her to her next leadership position. And her head of communications has no ulterior motive except to protect the CEO and the company from harm – what a win!

Working in a hierarchy

In Chapter 1, we talked about context, and how CEOs are expected to provide coherent responses to world events. It is the role of the CCO to help the CEO manage and respond to context. However, the specific context for the CEO/CCO relationship itself is that they exist in a power dynamic. The fact that the CEO or leader is on a higher rung in the workplace hierarchy can't be ignored as a dynamic in the relationship, and neither can its effect on trust.

Workplace pairs or dyads like the CEO and COO are quite common. What sets these two apart is that they are the only pair who interact solely and completely on the topic of reputation. It is important to have an awareness of the role of the hierarchy and how it affects how they relate. We can't ignore the power dynamics at work, and these are equally relevant for a C-Suite leader working with an executive communicator. It's unlikely that a leader and a communicator will ever be on the same level in the workplace hierarchy.

There are many frameworks in academic literature to understand power dynamics at work. The one that made the most sense to me is the framework of Leader-Member Exchange (LMX) referred to by Ferris, Liden and others which provides a further understanding of how attitudes, behaviours and outcomes are affected by these relationships in a power dynamic.[4]

Leader-Member Exchange (LMX) describes a relationship between a leader and a follower which contains many mutual aspects, such as 'affect, loyalty, contribution, professional respect, support, trust, attention, obligation, influence, delegation, latitude, and innovativeness.'[5] Since many of these themes emerged in the data from the interviews I held, LMX by name and by content provided some clues to understanding and decoding the CEO/CCO dyad.

The authors also describe 'high-quality connections' that involve 'mutual benefit, mutual influence, mutual expectation, and mutual understanding' that are characterized by trust. Interpersonal trust is important in terms of the CEO/CCO dyad, and this shows up in the data from the interviews. We have also seen that trust is a function of reputation. According to the authors, 'trust is arguably the most critical feature of virtually any kind of dyadic relationship,'[6] and trust, as we saw from Rachel Botsman and John Blakey in Chapter 5, derives from character and competence.

While much of the work of Ferris and Liden is too complex to cover here, a couple of important factors from their research include how workplace pairs develop increased trust, respect, affect and support, the roles of time, distance (both physical and psychological), and 'the controversial role of affect' in which dyadic pairs become too close to be objective.[7] In Robert Liden's further research, he also makes a salient point that even if one party in a dyad is of a higher status than the other, both are involved in the making of the relationship. Another aspect that is relevant are intention attributions, which 'tend to be positive when resources and support are freely exchanged.'[8] Relational leadership and trust play a joint role in which leaders begin to trust followers when they fulfilled tasks and roles successfully (competence), while followers trust leaders when they perceive they are being justly treated (character). CEOs and CCOs share a high 'task and outcome interdependence.'

What are the CEO and CCO's joint tasks?

We've seen that – unless they're in a state of reputational risk or repair – most CEOs and CCOs work on proactive reputation building, both for the company and for the CEO. Some of the respondents said that up to 90% of their work is proactive – a critical foundation against future reputational risk or crisis. So far, we've considered reputational risk as something that happens to a company, but it is also something that can happen to a person. As the 'face of the firm', CEOs will be held accountable when something goes wrong.[9]

CEOs need to build their own narrative moat – stories they tell about themselves, their personal history, experience, skills and what they've learned – to demonstrate who they are as a leader. This is highly relevant for diverse leaders, who may not have the buddy network inherent in the dominant workplace culture to tell everyone else why they are great for the job. While the network is very important, the onus may fall on diverse leaders to tell stories about themselves. And the CCO is their key partner here.

Notes on network and power

Angie believes the boys' club is still alive and based on outdated organizational structures created by men for men. In *Power*, Jeffrey Pfeffer devotes several pages to networking and how to get better at it.[10] Meg Bear's advice in building a leadership career is to invest in understanding and connecting more with power. She says she would have pushed back on this advice early in her career, but she now sees that it is important to 'invest in finding real sponsors and really powerful people who can help you break through.'

Meg says don't just focus on delivering outcomes for your manager; focus on connecting with many layers of power and be seen and known to as many layers of power to create opportunity. People might find this inauthentic or manipulative, but they can focus on how they deliver value to people more senior in the power structure. 'You are building relationships to offer value not to take something from them.' And this idea of offering value goes back to what Katja Kolmetz said about externalizing your value or effective telling.

In busy organizations, people aren't going to notice you unless you tell them why they should notice you. The power structures are unavoidable – just be smart, practice effective telling and find ways to be both visible and helpful to those in power.

Building coherence for target audiences as part of reputation management

CEOs and CCOs need to think of all audiences: employees, employee representatives or unions, board members, peers, investors, media, partners, customers, communities, academia, governments, non-governmental organizations and members of society.

Understanding the nuances of what all these different audiences want to see and hear from a leader is very hard to do alone. This is why a CCO is a vital partner – especially to a diverse CEO who is at risk from the glass cliff and a shorter tenure. In addition to character and competence, the two trust-building aspects the CCO brings to the CEO/CCO relationship, there is the important role of coherence.

The CCO helps the CEO build coherence around what to say when and to whom and consistency around how they show up. Sophie, one of the CEOs I interviewed, described this as 'code-switching.' She said she has over 40 engagements with different external audiences every month – without her head of executive communication as her partner in reminding her when to code-switch, she said she would be lost.

The Arthur W. Page Society is a global association for senior communications leaders. They produce regular practical guidebooks for CCOs, and they write to the Chief Communications Officer – an assumption that the head of communications is either on or very near to the C-Suite. The exclusivity of the organization combined with the C-Suite focus makes it aspirational. In my study of CCOs, of the 11 I interviewed, only four were C-Suite executives.

The Arthur W. Page Society's 2018 book, *The New Era of the CCO: The Essential Role of the CCO in a Volatile World*, edited by Bolton et al., has a chapter on working with the C-Suite.[11] The authors state that while the CEO sets direction, the CCO is most responsible for it being understood and acted upon – in the C-Suite and across the organization. The CEO is the executive responsible for creating alignment around shared strategic direction, business objectives with all audiences, and the CCO shares that responsibility.

The authors see the CCO as an integrator, but with a very important audience of one. To become highly trusted by the CEO, the CCO needs to build credibility by delivering communication activities that result in 'stakeholder buy-in and action' (that in turn secures the CEO's credibility with the Board or owners of the company).[12] To do so, the CCO also needs to collaborate with other C-Suite members, connecting their activities to the overall business drivers. In another chapter on corporate culture, the authors state that 'The CCO should act as the corporate conscience in the enterprise, advising CEOs and management on the ethics of its actions.'[13]

The work of the Arthur W. Page Society frames an ideal situation for CCOs and highlights their relevance to the CEO as 'corporate conscience.' It is much easier for CCOs to play this role if they report directly to the CEO. Sadly, this is not always the case.

What is the CCO remit and reporting line?

With all these audiences in mind, the CCO's remit is challenging and often broad. CCOs run the traditional reputation management function of PR, but many of those I spoke to also run internal communications, some run branding, analyst relations and government relations. One CCO had the entire sustainability function of the business in her organization, which is perhaps a trend we will see more of.

CCOs sit on their company's crisis management committees, and also work closely with leaders other than the CEO. Four of the 11 respondents are on the company leadership team which enables them to respond to the potential reputational risk of business decisions when they are being made. Those who are further away from the CEO in the organization need to work harder to get access, which adds to their emotional labour as they essentially have relationships with two bosses to maintain.

Factors in a good CEO/CCO relationship

There are two parts to this relationship – the *what* and the *how*. The *what* is what you work on together, the content. I'll address this in Part 3. This chapter is the *how*. Many leaders and CEOs neglect the how (believe me, communicators know and complain about it all the time) which leads to them scratching their heads about what their CCO does.

I was in a workshop with the CEO of a communications technology start-up. They build tech for communicators to thrive at work. He said to me, 'I don't know what my communicators do all day.' If a CEO who focuses on helping communicators doesn't know what their communicators are doing, then they are neglecting the how. And this means their communicators are probably doing tactical not strategic work (the what).

My research shows how to fix the how, and the key word is trust. Respondents who report good trust, whether explicit or implicit, report a good relationship with their CEO or CCO. Trust is a vital ingredient in a relationship that exists continuously in the pervasive context of reputational risk. Without trust, the CEO and CCO are not able to function whether proactively or reactively. It is a critical filter.

Building trust is not about being present and being a good person. It is possible to be both those things in a reputational risk situation and fail to manage it. There are three vital trust-building factors that must be fulfilled: time and space (managed by the CEO), courage/impact (responsibility of the CCO), and competence/intentionality (demonstrated by the CCO). If these aspects are in place – and both actors are conscious of their responsibilities in managing and prosecuting them – the CEO and CCO stand in good stead to manage and mitigate reputational risk.

These are the ideal aspects. Some of the interviewees were lucky enough to fulfil all of these, and both the CEO and the CCO reported high trust.

The CEO's trust-building responsibilities

In the reputation play, where the CEO is main actor, she, he or they is often also the director. The director manages the rehearsal space and times. Time is manifest in the CEO/CCO relationship in both length of tenure and amount of time they spend in each other's company. Ferris calls space 'distance' and says it can be both physical and psychological.[14] Communicators tend to mix time and space together and call it 'access' but I treat them separately to demonstrate to CEOs how intentional they need to be in building this aspect of the relationship.

Many of the CCOs I interviewed said they need more time with the CEO. However, those who report directly to the CEO, either as members of the leadership team or not, do not claim a need for more time. Those who report to an intermediary, such as the head of marketing or HR, are less satisfied with how much time they have with the CEO. Of those who report directly, only one wanted more time and this was in the context of timeliness of response.

CCOs who work in the same location as the CEO report less dissatisfaction about the amount of time they have together. They report having 'walk-in rights' and 'popping in' or 'bumping into him in the corridor.' Simon Paris is CEO of Finastra, one of the world's largest fintech companies. Simon, who is not co-located with his head of communications, said his 90% informal communication is 'not great' (this was not a denigration of the CCO, just a reflection that more formal time was needed). Sean, a CEO who has a 20-plus year working relationship with the CCO – that they separately described as almost ideal – said that even their work tempo or cadence was sometimes out of synch.

If physical distance cannot be overcome, CEOs need to think about psychological distance. Unavailability or unresponsiveness creates a psychological distance that challenges the foundation of trust. CCOs might start to fill in the gaps with suppositions about why the CEO is being unresponsive. In LMX, Liden et al., call these intention attributions, which 'tend to be positive when resources and support are freely exchanged.'[15]

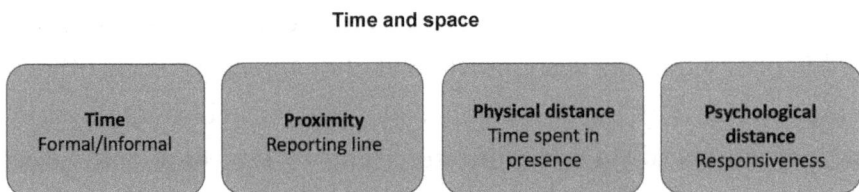

Time and space

Time Formal/Informal	Proximity Reporting line	Physical distance Time spent in presence	Psychological distance Responsiveness

Figure 2: The CEO's trust-building responsibilities

It is not necessary (and often not possible) to have all four factors in place. The most trusting and (self-reportedly) successful CEO/CCO relationships have at least three. Three respondents report having all four factors, and also report very high trust. In one of those cases, I also interviewed the CEO and her reported level of trust matched that of the CCO. CCO respondents who do not report to the CEO and do not have physical proximity all say they need more time. In one case, all four factors are in place, but the CCO still reports lack of trust. This is because the psychological distance is increased by the CEO behaviours of backtracking and changing the goalposts.

To build trust to manage and mitigate reputational risk, the CEO needs to take responsibility for the factors of time and space. Thanks to the hierarchy and power differential at play in organizations, CCOs cannot control how much formal or informal time they have with the CEO, their reporting line or the physical or psychological distance. This is the choice of the CEO, and CEOs need to manage this consciously.

If they wish their CCO to continue reporting to the CMO or the CHRO, then they need to ensure they compensate with time and responsiveness. If they cannot overcome physical distance, they need to put more formal time in the calendar. If all four factors are not fulfilled, a CCO might start to make intention attributions (he does not value my work; she thinks I am not good enough). Whether these are true or not is irrelevant; the attributions fill in the time and space gaps.

CCOs often use texting as a proxy to overcome physical or psychological distance, but I saw that texting can be a double-edged sword. In a working relationship of long tenure, where understanding and communication have been built over time, texting can serve as a useful shorthand. One CCO who has all four time and space factors in place rarely uses texting as a means of communication with the CEO and reports that he is 'relieved' about this. Another CCO reports that texting became such a useful shorthand for closeness and access that her personal development was forgotten.

If CEOs make conscious choices about the four time and space factors, and even articulate their choices to the CCO, they are creating opportunities to build trust. The CCO can then play his, her or their role in building trust to manage reputational risk.

The CCO's trust-building responsibilities

CCOs operate within a corporate hierarchy, where their main partner in the work dyad is the CEO of the company. In LMX theories, Liden et al., state that even if one party in a dyad is of a higher status than the other, both are involved in the making of the relationship. And this is even more important since the CEO/CCO dyad has a high task/outcome interdependence – success for the CEO is success for the CCO and vice versa.[16] I would suggest from my dataset that the CCO's ability to deliver high-quality tasks provides the CEO with excellent outcomes in the context of reputation management. And the CEO's ability to give attribution where it is due for the high-quality tasks inspires more trust.

Sometimes in the CEO/CCO dyad, the CCO takes control of the show and becomes director. In reputation terms, this means giving advice or counsel about the reputational risk of a business decision or a particular leadership stance. In the dataset this is described variously as 'holding up a mirror,' 'speaking truth to power,' 'doing what is right for the company' and 'feedback,' and there are several examples of this in Chapter 9. It's also about helping the CEO or the executive build coherence in the contested context in which they work.

The conundrum here is that the CCO needs trust to fulfil this, but also builds trust by fulfilling it. If the time and space factors are in place, the CCO will be able to courageously provide the necessary feedback. Lisa describes how she has counselled the CEO against an action (and later been thanked for it). Her time and space factors are well-fulfilled (she has several formal meetings with the CEO, reports directly to him and has an open invitation to attend any Board meetings she sees fit). Providing counsel is harder to do without time and space factors, since it is impossible to advise someone who is absent.

LMX research shows that workplace pairs can become too close to be objective. Liam talks about remembering who pays his salary, while Lisa reflects on having been too close to other CEOs in the past. Sean says that the CCO helps him avoid the 'reality distortion field' and that he values her judgment, objectivity and 'intellectual honesty.'

Avoiding bias and providing objective counsel are key roles CCOs provide to build trust for the management and mitigation of reputational risk. These take courage, and character, but in all these cases, time and space functions are fulfilled.

This aspect of the relationship requires both the CEO and the CCO. There is another aspect that is entirely the role of the CCO. I call this intentionality.

CCO's responsibility: managing with intention

It's clear that in order to be a good CCO, a person needs a wide range of skills and competencies. One of the things that became extremely clear during the interviews was how much consideration CCOs give to managing the relationship with the CEO to help them be more efficient, make faster decisions and be more effective in their roles. The CCO is a CEO learning machine, constantly taking feedback, and improving his, her or their output.

Themes that emerged were around matching the CEO style, knowing when to approach the CEO, how to approach the CEO, when to rely on others, being a safe space for the CEO, managing the information flow and managing their own (the CCO's) emotions.

The fact that Abigal, a head of communications who sits on the board, says 'the most important thing is no surprises' is interesting, because while it appears to mean telling the CEO everything, what she really intends here is only telling the CEO the things that could be important. There is a filtering or sieving function at play.

Both Abigail and Lisa articulate that the CCO thinks much more about the role than the CEO does. Lisa says it is the responsibility of the CCO to manage the relationship (she calls it 'interface') in a way 'that suits the CEO best and listen and, of course, correct along the way.' She describes working for different CEOs and matching her style accordingly. Abigail says 'most of the initiative comes from the head of comms.'

By managing the relationship, course correcting and improving, the CCO builds trust with the CEO. This aspect is easier to manage without properly fulfilled time and space needs than the aspect of courage and impact.

High task/outcome interdependence

Requires time and space considerations from the CEO

Character
Acting with courage

Competence
Being intentional

Figure 3: The COO's trust-building responsibilities

The Relationship between the CEO and the CCO

As we've seen, the CEO's trust-building responsibilities are around creating time and space for the relationship to grow and trust to build, while the CCO's responsibility is around demonstrating competence and character. (If you think back to Chapter 5, competence and character are two key factors in reputation.) It gets a bit meta, but in order to build company and the CEO's reputation, the CCO needs to demonstrate a reputation for being trustworthy. And the CEO needs to give that reputation time and space to flourish.

If all aspects are in place the CCO can act with character and competence to help the CEO create coherence, manage reputation-building and mitigate reputational risk.

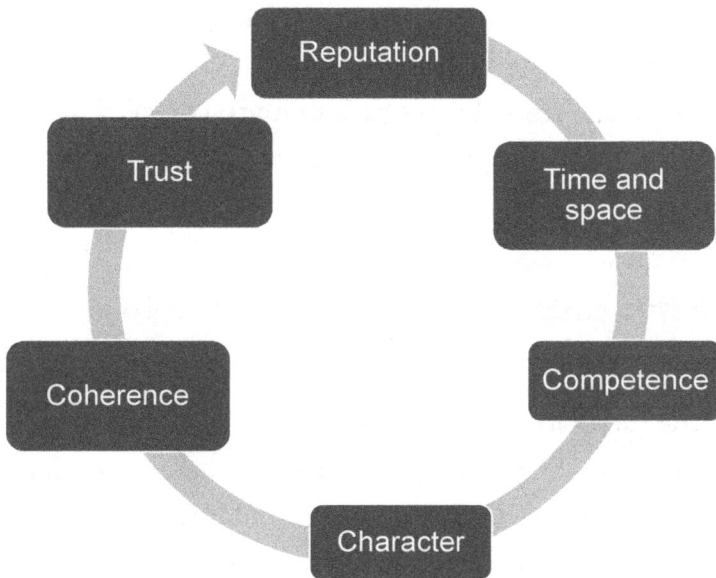

Figure 4: How the CEO and CCO build trust to manage reputation

Conclusion

The importance of the CEO and CCO relationship has been under-estimated as part of the reputation story. If you look at the Arthur W. Page Society book referenced in this chapter, you can tell that CCOs know how important it is. The CEOs I interviewed verbalize the importance of the relationship, but some don't actually put the conditions in place to ensure that the trust is built. CEOs need to give their CCOs time and space so that the relationship can grow, so that they can build both CEO and company reputation proactively against future crisis – and work as a well-oiled, effective team when crisis hits.

CEOs operate in and have to make sense of complex contexts. If they have chosen a CCO of character and competence, who can help them create coherence for their many audiences, both their own and their company's reputations will be upheld. But the onus is also on them, the CEO, to ensure the right conditions are in place for that CCO's character and competence to shine through. You cannot advise someone you never see.

And for CEOs from diverse backgrounds: you get a relationship with someone who has no ulterior motive other than to see you succeed.

From this chapter: Lessons in leadership communication

- The career longevity of CEOs from URM is threatened.
- Diverse CEOs may not have the buddy network of non-diverse CEOs so reputation building is critical.
- Their CCO is the best possible partner to build a personal narrative moat against personal crisis, as well as a company narrative moat against company crisis.
- To achieve this, CEOs from URM need to build trust with their CCOs.
- Not doing both is risky and a wasted opportunity – CEOs from URM need to lean on their CCO or head of communications to ensure their reputation is viable and portable.

Part 3

New reputation equity

Researchers have studied the relationship between reputation and future equity for businesses. Failure to build personal reputation equity can cost CEOs and leaders from diverse backgrounds future career success. Leaning on a CCO or head of communications helps leaders think actively about reputation, whether they are CEOs, senior managers or founders. This helps us build a cohort of new leaders who are better equipped to manage the challenges that lie ahead.

Chapter 9

Creating your reputation equity

In the last chapter we looked at the ideal situation for a CEO and CCO pair to work on a basis of trust to build reputation. By creating a safe space and building a relationship (the how), you develop a unique environment to work on your reputation equity (the what).

Researchers have shown that for businesses, good reputations lead to lower levels of future equity, while bad reputations lead to higher equity.[1]

Why this matters for leaders from diverse backgrounds

In Chapter 1, we talked about the challenging context for leaders, in which they constantly have to navigate if, when and how to respond to world events. Your CCO can be your trusted partner for this, providing counsel on your response.

They help you build coherence, which is a vital part of your reputation equity. Coherence can be in response to world events, it can be around how you communicate to your teams, and it can be around how you show up personally. Coherence is about creating meaning.

In human terms, the lower cost of equity associated with a good leadership reputation could mean a higher perceived trust, greater autonomy and visibility, more leadership opportunities and sustained career progression.

As your reputation manager, your CCO will help you define what you stand for and what you want to be known for, they will tie your personal story to the strategy of the business and encourage you to use narratives in an authentic way. A reputation manager takes this work seriously – we've seen how intentional the CCO is about showing up for the CEO or leader and about keeping information confidential. This is where you work on use of language and how you create meaning for all audiences who are looking to you as the leader to provide perspective and direction. The CCO might encourage you to talk about things you might not find important, but trust the process, because they are experts in hunting down the reputational diamonds to help you sparkle. And, if you create the right conditions for trust to grow, it is in this safe space where you will receive honest feedback.

What honest feedback looks like

Eileen, who heads communications at a large German multinational, describes how she learned two days into her job that the CEO wanted unvarnished feedback:

> 'When I joined... it was earnings, and we had this internal format where he addresses all employees... Afterwards, he asked me for feedback and now obviously, I was very diplomatic having been socialized in a more political company. And he says, "Well, yeah, thanks a lot. I get it. But now tell me what you really think."'

This is an important point: companies that are political make giving feedback harder. This is why the trust dynamic matters so much. Even within the swirl of company politics, your CCO should feel safe enough to tell you what they really think. Your reputation might depend on it. As a leader, asking for genuine feedback is a key part of creating an inclusive culture, as we saw in Chapter 2.

Asking hard questions

Donald Kau is head of communications and PR at a company that manages a major African tourist destination. He more than once described his role in the leadership team (where he sits but does not hold an executive title) as being able to ask the hard questions: 'And even when I question (the CEO's) thinking, he does allow me in the executive meetings, to probably get away with being a little bit more pushy in asking questions.'

He explains later when talking about crisis management why this role is important to the CEO and other executives:

'Because I'm in the room, I can sometimes ask a difficult question before it's asked by a hostile journalist who's at the door. What you're just doing is testing if they've applied their mind to potential risk issues that could play out as communication or reputational issues.'

Donald says he is cautious about calling everything a crisis – he says if he did so too often, the CEO and executive team would lose trust in him. However, what he says here is interesting: it is his role to pressure test executive decisions for reputational risk behind closed doors. And it's the trust that he and the CEO have built over years that allows him to play that role.

Avoiding the echo chamber

Amanda, who is a CCO in a tech company, talked about the echo chamber effect: 'Most executives, you know, they end up in a bit of an echo chamber of their own making.' She says it is her role to manage that. The CEO she works with, Sean, also talks about the echo chamber when he says:

> 'three things I've learned about being a CEO is number one the day you become CEO, you become 50% funnier. And the second thing is the truth becomes 50% more opaque. That's the second thing and then the third is the number of people willing to be direct with you reduces by 50%... It's just a function of the role. People just tend to behave that way.'

He says he appreciates his CCO's 'intellectual honesty' and her ability to give him a perspective on 'the state of things without value judgment.'

Amanda also said that in managing the relationship with the CEO to protect company reputation, CCOs must be prepared to deliver bad news:

> 'I think you be prepared to be super honest and take the backlash that could come from that CEOs... They certainly don't love to hear bad news about themselves or their companies. But it doesn't do anybody any good if you're sort of sugar-coating or massaging the message of something that is true reputational risk.'

Remembering who they serve

When talking about managing reputational risk in tandem with the CEO, the FTSE 50 CCO says:

> 'We have a relationship of trust. They know that I'm on their side. I'm Team (company). I'm Team (CEO). And I think it's important to say both of those things, because candidly, if it comes down to it, (CEO) doesn't pay my paycheck... My job is (company) not (CEO).'

Lisa, who runs communications at a large global technology conglomerate echoed this when she said she has 'a very big duty not to please (the CEO), but to serve (the company).' She describes three situations in her career where she's written the CEO an email to challenge decisions that she believes will either affect his or the company's reputation. She knows that the CEO appreciates this: 'sometimes we've had very difficult conversations and he's appreciated that I've stood my ground and I'm passionate.'

Lisa says that she believes it's her job to 'share the honest truth. So, I think that that's... key to be a bit of a voice of the organization, to hold a bit of a mirror up.'

Avoiding bias and the reality distortion field

While having access and trust pave the way for the CCO to be the mirror, give feedback, speak truth to power or have the hard discussions, there is a very real danger of becoming too close. Lisa says:

> 'I think it's a fine line between building trust and respect and becoming too close, so you can't, you can no longer be unbiased to support them. And I mean, I've found myself getting close to that in different situations. And so now I actually think it's really important that you manage it so you're always doing the right thing for the company and for the individual.'

I see courage here, and CEOs are aware of this emotionally courageous role that the CCO must play. Simon Paris said it was clear to him that the CCO 'is very confident to speak truth to power' and give feedback. Sophie said, 'I'm making sure I'm acting on the guidance given by (my CCO), hey how would you want to formulate a certain, take a certain stance, and hey, don't do that.' A third

CEO told me it's important for him to work with someone who has 'a point of view.'

Sean, a CEO, explained that it is the CCO's role to help the CEO avoid the reality distortion field:

> 'If the CEO has an agenda and it's just blasting propaganda for the head of comms to parrot to the market, then that's an unhealthy relationship. I think intellectual honesty where the CEO can share their aspirations, dreams, hopes, excitement about the company and the market and where you want to go absolutely. But, at the same time, I think CEOs can very quickly land in a reality distortion field, either because they're not hearing reality from people or they just choose to live in it, whatever that may be.'

This speaks back to Professor Linda Hill's concept of creative abrasion that leads to innovation. If there is not a willingness for the CCO to be straightforward in their opinions with the CEO, then the CEO is choosing a path of less innovation.

I often say to executives, 'Do you want the honest answer or the political answer?' and then give them both. This helps executive to understand the gap between spin and reality in order to find the path that is best for them.

Being intentional

One of the bigger themes that became extremely clear during the research was how much consideration CCOs give to managing the relationship with the CEO to help them be more efficient, make faster decisions and be more effective in their roles. The CCO is a CEO learning machine, constantly taking feedback, and improving his, her or their output. This is part of their capability reputation.

Lisa explained this aspect of the relationship in more depth when she says:

> 'And what's so interesting is it's not such a two-way street, in my experience, because they are the CEO, and no matter how empowering and respectful they are, they've got such a massive role. And so I manage how I interact in multiple different ways according to the style of the CEO. So whether that's been very structured as I am today, with my CEO or being completely ad hoc with somebody who prefers that style. I think it's on the comms head to manage it in the way that suits the CEO best and listen and, of course, correct along the way.'

Onus on the CCO

Abigail, who sat on the board and had been a former peer of the CEO before he was promoted, holds the same view. She says while there are two people in the relationship and it is an important one, 'most of the initiative comes from the head of comms, not the CEO who is simply too busy with all kinds of other stuff.'

In giving advice to communicators, CEO Simon Paris describes this as the 'relentless need to keep yourself front of mind for the CEO. They will forget, they will get distracted by the day to day and they will lurch from one burning platform to another and not bring you up to speed with what they are thinking about.'

Knowing when and how to approach the CEO

Ulrike holds an executive position on the Executive Management team of her company and reports directly to the CEO. She describes how, having worked together for six years, she knows the CEO very well. This knowledge means: 'I know when to approach him and what he expects. I also know how to approach him in the most effective way.' She says the CEO 'likes people to be very well-prepared,' but she understands when and how to be formal when communicating with him and when not: 'I know where I need to have a pre-read, I need to have a presentation or briefing ready and on time, and I know which topics can be discussed in a less formal way and maybe on my way to a meeting or when we are traveling. So, I do like that balance.'

Part of this dance is about knowing when to involve the CEO: 'That full accessibility so that I could call him and be in touch anytime that I very much feel I know, he knows which decisions I can take by myself and which decisions he should be a part of.'

Karen Quinn is senior director of corporate communications at Finastra, one of the world's largest fintech companies. She says that when working on a crisis, she is especially aware when and how to involve CEO Simon Paris. 'I think the fact that he can trust me to work on something and then involve him when I need to, so that I am not constantly being a drain.'

Amanda, who has worked with the CEO for nearly 20 years also thinks deeply about how and when to involve him:

'I don't come to him with this is the problem. What do you think we should do?... I come to him and say, this is the ask and here's what we're going to do or here's what I think we should do or here's how I would approach it and that accomplishes two things, right. One is obviously not asking him to solve problems. But the second is it gives him something to react to which I always say it's easier to edit than create.'

Abigail underscores this knowledge when she says:

'And what I did with comms was more towards you know, the external reputational risks, but I usually didn't mention them in the board unless there was something that everybody needed to, to be aware of. And that was mostly in the sense that, yes, we know something is going on. Yes, we know that. Your employees will talk about when I talk about it, the please tell them then to not respond to not engage this will go away.'

This thoughtfulness is also reflected in how CCOs learn to match the CEO's style.

Matching the CEO's style

CEO Sophie says her CCO is 'plugged into my way of thinking, and how I would approach it.' Mike Ettling, a CEO whom we met in Chapter 6, says his CCO 'pretty effectively learned my voice.' Karen says her four-year working relationship with CEO Simon means 'I am in his head, so I know what he's thinking.' She elaborates: 'I seem to have lost my own personality in that I think like Simon and I write like Simon and none of it's me.'

Prenessa says that matching the CEO's style is about ensuring that tone is right, and that she is using inclusive language. She also believes it's important to understand not only the CEO's vision for the business, but their vision for themselves. She needs to know 'where the leader is going or what the aspiration is so I can support and influence in that particular manner.'

Lisa describes this having no agenda. 'I say this to my CEO: my agenda is to advance your agenda. My business is your business.' For one CCO this means 'knowing what makes this person tick as a person.'

Being a safe space for the CEO

Liam describes how during times of reputational risk, he provides a safe space for the CEO ('they can vent, and they can ask questions').

He is the only CCO who mentions that CEOs often take their CCOs with them when they change roles (this is implicit but not expressed in the 20-year relationship between one CEO/CCO pair who have worked together at several companies).

He also told me that the CEO:

'is our principal actor in the stakeholder engagement play. And so consequently, being supported and being advised incredibly well in that space is so important to the success of that CEO and the success of the business. So I think that that relationship is so critical and it's why so often it's a very personal appointment. It's why when someone moves companies, you'll often find they'll appear with the person ready to get on with them with the person who did this gig in the previous place.'

Managing the information flow

Lisa splits information flow between what's for information, decision or discussion in order to use time with her CEO as effectively as possible. Abigail manages information to share with the CEO: 'I would also sometimes do this like you know, heads up, this is going on, I'm not asking for advice, but I just want you to know and be aware, in case someone asks you about it, you know that it is under control, and it's been taken care of.'

She also says, 'The most important thing I think personally in this relationship is no surprises.'

Donald Kau describes this process of knowing which information to share when as 'building context for them,' in which he describes to the leadership team and the CEO how he is thinking about potential reputational risks. He also warns that CCOs need to be cautious about what they flag as risky, because 'overdoing it can be tiring for them, and can be dispiriting for you if at some point, they don't take you seriously.' He describes this as avoiding becoming the boy who cried wolf.

What happens when it goes wrong

Two things can happen when it goes wrong. If trust has not been built in all the ways I've described, the pair will be less prepared and less able to manage a risk or crisis situation when it arises. We know that reputations are easy to lose, and if a CEO and CCO have not built trust and an effective way of working, the crisis management will be substantially harder.

The other thing that can go wrong is that the CCO will leave. While one had all the time and space considerations in place, the fact that the CEO kept changing the goalposts and refused to be the face of the company at a time of reputational risk was causing trust issues for her. Another CCO, who was a highly respected industry veteran, was not getting enough time with CEO, which caused her frustration.

How to fix it

If a CEO has a sense that a CCO is frustrated, they need to take a long look at how they are treating them. They need to ensure that they are spending enough formal time with their CCO, and not just having informal contact. Perhaps they need to take another look at the reporting line. If the CEO and CCO are not co-located or if the company works completely remotely, the CEO needs to ensure that they overcome the physical distance by creating psychological closeness.

If the CEO is frustrated with the CCO's performance, they need to look to themselves. Have they created the conditions for this person to thrive? If not, first fix those. If they change the conditions and are still frustrated then the CEO and CCO are not a good match, and it is time to make a change.

If a CCO is frustrated, they do need to articulate to the CEO what the problem is. CEOs have a lot to manage and being transparent about the problem will help.

I have created a checklist of questions for the CEO and the CCO to ask themselves to assess their relationship, and see if it is in a good place to manage and mitigate reputational risk. You will find these in the Resources section at the end of the book.

What to look for when hiring

Getting the match right at the beginning will help avoid some of these problems. In the Resources section I have a checklist of questions for HR, the CEO and the CCO to ask themselves during the hiring process.

Conclusion

Your CCO is the only leader on the team whose full responsibility it is to manage company and CEO reputation. (And if it isn't, you should task them with it.) The rest of your leadership team are prosecuting their own roles, whether it's marketing, finance, sales, product or HR. They may have opinions on reputation, but it is not the entire gamut of their function. Reputation is an intangible asset that is hard to build, easy to lose and costly when you do lose it. When you become a leader or CEO, you neglect reputation and the relationship with your CCO at your own cost. This can be a safe space for you to get the feedback and advice you need to build your own reputation – one that helps you land the next big leadership role – and create the coherence, capability and character that forms your own reputation equity.

From this chapter: Lessons in leadership communication

- Role-play crisis possibilities behind the safety of closed doors – it will make you much better prepared when crisis hits and journalists are asking for answers.
- Build a reputation strategy with your CCO or executive communicator, revisit it every quarter and don't be afraid to take risks and experiment.
- Recognize and thank your CCO or head of communication for their unseen labour – it is all in the service of your and your company's reputation.
- Communicators should not just be aspiring to be reputation managers – CEOs should create a relationship of trust with CCOs so that CCOs know they have the mandate to fully own company and CEO reputation.

Chapter 10

Reputation equity for non-CEOs

Not everyone is a CEO. This chapter is for diverse leaders, whether senior or emerging, who want to build their reputation to secure the next senior role. If CCOs are helping CEOs demonstrate character, competence and the ability to build coherence to shore up their reputations, this chapter talks about some people other leaders can lean on and some tools they can use to grow a reputation that speaks for itself.

How you manage this process depends on where you are in the organization, and your career, and what kind of budget you have. It also depends on how determined you are, and how much you care about your reputation.

Why this matters for leaders from diverse backgrounds

We've seen the statistics in Chapter 2 about how poor the diversity is in the C-Suite. Yes, there's been progress but not nearly enough to truly represent employee and societal demographics on boards and senior leadership teams. Meg Bear talked about her ambition to land a board role and how she went about gaining the skills she needed. In addition to the skills, she mentioned that it's very important as a leader to be seen and known as a whole person.

Diverse leaders are consistently spoken over in meetings and taken less seriously.[1] A strong platform in which you are recognized both inside and outside the company as an authority cannot be argued with or spoken over. By building your reputation, you define and say what you stand for before others can.

This goes back to the luck surface area in Chapter 6: doing the work is not enough. You need to be enthusiastically and consistently talking about the work. Mary Ann Sieghart's research in *The Authority Gap* shows that 'a 'superb' record of achievement can definitely act as a 'buffer against bias.'[2]

Kholi talks about this as 'not dimming your lights.' She told me about a leader she had at Accenture who encouraged her to speak up:

> 'I came from an audit background and, you know, we are so intuitive, we listen and we don't want to be talking just for the sake of talking. You listen with intent to understand and respond. And he came to me one time and he said, "You're quiet." And I said, yes, there was no reason for me to say anything in that meeting, because I think the context was covered. And he says that "the problem is you're not visible. People don't see you. You've got to talk, even if you're repeating what someone else said."'

She later passed that same advice on to a female colleague:

> 'It was when I was a manager in the audit firm, there was a woman who was so quiet that no-one wanted to engage with her. She would be given a section to deliver on, and then once she was done, she would sit in a corner and not say she's finished. And I sat with her and I discovered that she was finishing seven hours of work in four hours. Everyone was transferring her to other projects because they could not work with her. And I asked her why didn't you come

and share that you've done so that we can get you another project? Then she understood how she could have been more visible, to be able to be seen, to be doing something, rather than sitting there, not doing anything. And after that, she became an excellent leader and has her own company now.'

Meg's point about audiences in leadership reflects the audiences you focus on as you build your reputation equity. And you can work with a communicator or reputation manager to help you do this.

Who's on your reputation team

Start with the CCO. If you're a member of the C-Suite, it is the responsibility of the CCO to ensure that you're getting at least some communications support. While it's unlikely the CCO will have the time or the bandwidth to be your reputation manager themselves, they will either have an executive communications team that can support you or nominate someone who is interested in doing so.

When I ran executive communications, we supported the entire board or C-Suite, as well as certain very senior leaders. Our internal reputation was so good we were constantly asked to provide executive communications support to other leaders, and quite often had to say no because we didn't have enough bandwidth ourselves.

If the CCO and the executive communications team can't support you, try the CMO. It's in marketing's interests to have a number of senior leaders apart from the CEO who provide thought leadership. In B2B especially, people buy from people and the marketing function will be grateful to have someone who can put their names to blogs and videos that present the product to the market. Marketing also has more budget than communications, and they will be able to find and fund events for you to speak at.

If you're running a function with a large budget, you can hire your own executive communicator (EC). Make sure you run this past the CCO first, and use the lists in the Resources chapter to ensure that you match with someone who is a good fit.

Mistakes to avoid

One of the mistakes I often find leaders make when they hire their own EC is they are often too busy to meet with them. They use their chief of staff as an intermediary. Your chief of staff is not you! If you are too busy to meet with your EC a couple of times a month, then you are too busy to have one, and they will end up frustrated and either leave or check out.

Not building a relationship with your EC – the way the CEO and CCO build a relationship – is entirely counterproductive and equivalent to throwing money out of the window. Hire an EC if you care about building a relationship with your communicator; not to be a nice person but to build a genuine reputation. If you hire an EC and they're only meeting your chief of staff, then you're performing reputation management and the way you show up (whether it's on LinkedIn or internally) will look fake.

Insight: Value of regular meetings

I worked with an executive who was not shy about telling me how much he disliked communications. However, he met with me regularly, and by getting to know him better I was able to find and create communications opportunities for him that were a good match to his communications style. If we'd never met, and the relationship had been filtered through his chief of staff, I would never have reached that level of understanding and I would have continued to make suggestions that he hated. Knowing him as a person helped me improve his reputation and standing as a leader.

Find a coach

If it's too much of a financial outlay to hire a full-time employee, you can always work with a reputation or communications coach. You can look for someone on LinkedIn. Make sure you check out their website and recommendations to ensure that they are genuine and have the kind of experience you're looking for.

You can also define how long you want the engagement to be and what you want to get out of it. I've worked as an executive communications coach on engagements that last over two years and some that are only a month long. It depends what your goals are, and a good coach will recognize and be respectful of that.

If you care deeply about your reputation and want to develop it but don't have disposable budget, the next section will help you think through some elements of reputation that you can work on yourself.

What are your reputation tools?

Waller and Younger say there are three dice in the reputation game: behaviours, networks and narratives.[3] They say how you behave or act sends signals to others about what they can expect from you. However, you can't control everything about your reputation because it is filtered through networks. The networks you choose to engage in tell people how to read your reputation. And third, how you use narratives about yourself will influence your reputation.

These three things – behaviours, networks and narratives – were strongly threaded through all of the interviews with diverse leaders in preparing to write this book. Whether consciously or not, they are all employing these to manage their reputations.

However, since diverse leaders come from such varied and diverse backgrounds, and have different identities, there is baseline work that comes first.

Knowing yourself

All of the interviewees demonstrated deep self-knowledge. Having coaching or therapy can help with gaining self-knowledge. In fact, David, whom you might remember as the non-binary leader from Chapter 3, advises emerging leaders to 'work on yourself and heal your traumas, otherwise they will block you as a leader.' Jack Nugent is a leader who grew up in poverty in London, went to Cambridge and then into the City (a term for the part of London that is one of the financial centres of the world). He acknowledges that his need for financial security informed all the career decisions he made. To Jack, 'poverty is not an absolute, consistent state but an everchanging volatile ride of peaks and troughs.' He's observed others from more privileged backgrounds and seen how easy it is for them to be both carefree and entitled in a business context, given the safety net they can always fall back on. He also talked about the professional codes that he was unaware of and had to learn in order to progress his career.

Knowing your unique identity

Peter Figge is the CEO and co-owner of the renowned German advertising agency Jung von Matt. He is very clear on how his personality – and who he is as a gay man – reflects in his leadership style. He knows, and has had feedback from others, that he consistently treats all people in the same way, shows up as the same person no matter what room he is in, and communicates in a consistent way. He says that this kind of personal understanding is key to leadership: 'I strongly believe that in leadership, if you don't have a functioning system of your self assessment and perception from the outside, then you cannot be a good leader. If you don't know how people perceive you, you will not be able to be a meaningful leader.'

Part of that understanding is knowing how your identity affects your leadership style. Peter says his consistency as a leader stems from his identity:

> 'As a gay person, for example, you just are forced to reflect more on stuff, becoming yourself. So you either become distracted, or, if you have the strength of somebody who is helping you to really sort of deal with yourself, then you are forced much earlier, to also develop certain things. By default, you realize that there is just not any other option than to be yourself if you want to become a halfway happy person.'

For Tony Jamous, CEO of software company Oyster whom we met in Chapter 6, says that deep self-understanding is an important step towards finding purpose: 'So step number one, how you become more in touch with your inner self and your inner experience, is by becoming more and more sensitive.' Here Tony talks about techniques for getting in touch with oneself, such as meditation, yoga and mindfulness. 'Once you become more and more sensitive to what's going on inside of you, and the second step, is to choose what to do with that information, that signalling. And to choose, you have to be clear about why you're here, your purpose.'

By embracing your inner self, you celebrate your own uniqueness. This is something Kholi told me when she talked about not losing her identity:

> 'If I emulate your style or the style of a man, I lose my identity when I get to the boardroom and where I could potentially focus as myself – with my expertise – I lose it because I'm fighting the game of wanting to be like you or wanting to be like that other leader in that classical leadership style. If you can bring your uniqueness to the boardroom, you effect

change, and are able to sustain your role and be comfortable with who you are.'

Self-understanding, and a consciousness around identity, is the key first step to building a reputation and being a good leader. There may be some work to do in terms of coaching or therapy to get to that place of understanding. Many of the diverse leaders I interviewed described a process of getting over obstacles.

Case study: Learning from a major reset

Antonia Ashton is a single mother who runs a large global team of over 100 people in a tech company. In a sense, her obstacle was herself. She describes how, between 2001 and 2012, she suffered burnout twice through overwork and credits this to perfectionism. The two burnouts, combined with her strong urge to become a parent, led to a complete reset. She exchanged her large management role for a smaller one and moved back to her home country, South Africa. In 2014, after several rounds of IVF, her daughter was born:

> 'This began a very different chapter of my leadership journey. Some of the expectations I had around being a working mother, and a leader came to fruition, and other things surprised me.'

Antonia says that having a child has helped her manage her stress better because children require you to be present. After a long week at work, she can't take to the sofa and watch Netflix; she needs to be present, available and doing the things her child needs her to do. She has now found that being mindfully present with her daughter doing activities together is a better way to recharge than a weekend on the sofa. She is also highly aware that her child can soak up her stress by osmosis and to avoid that, she has had to find ways to manage it so that it does not leak through. And, as a single parent, she has had to create very clear boundaries between work and family time:

> 'Another gift that being a single mother within the professional environment, that a person with a partner might not necessarily have, is that I've had to be unequivocal about drawing lines in the sand. There is no-one else to bath her or read stories to her. There is no one else. I cannot do calls from six until half past eight in the evenings. And that's been a gift for me because it's also taught me when you unequivocally say I won't be available, people at work accept that.'

Behaviour

As Antonia's story shows, self-knowledge leads to consistent behaviour. Based on his own inner work, Tony says he 'created an environment where everybody is invited to be their true self... how I create the psychological safety is by being less reactive or non-reactive to bad news, by defaulting to trust and defaulting to assuming best intent.'

Tony's radical self-acceptance leads to a radical acceptance of others which leads to a highly innovative culture:

> 'I thrive on making people feel safe with me. The impact of that is that I become a much more approachable leader. I stop being a threat, or less of a threat, because I cannot solve everything... So first you become safer and therefore you make people feel more seen and heard, because they can suddenly open up to you. And that that flexibility also is powerful, because if people know that you're not going to

react to whatever's going to happen negatively, then they're not afraid of making mistakes. You end up creating more innovative cultures where mistakes are welcome or thought of as learning opportunities.'

Vania, who we met in Chapter 6, says that her leadership communication style is very direct, and she expects her team to be equally direct with her. 'I don't get nuances and if you are not direct, the chances for misinterpretation are very high.' As a CEO who has worked in various countries, including Indonesia, Azerbaijan and the UK, she realizes that in many cultures it's not acceptable to be direct with the boss.

'The first day I start work with a team I tend to set out my way of working so people know exactly what to expect. I think it's easier.' She welcomes confrontation or debates as ways to get to clarity: 'I believe that there are ways to level up misunderstanding and I really do prefer that. But I do recognize that not everyone enjoys confrontation, so I try to be respectful about their preferences.'

However, by warning everyone upfront about her style, people are less likely to be shocked when it happens – and it cracks the door open for healthy debates to occur.

Reputation based on consistent behaviour is not limited to leaders, but also to the cultures they lead. Sara Daw, co-founder and group CEO of The Liberti group and The CFO Centre group, says the secret of the business that she and her business partner Colin have built up over the years is in connecting with their people. 'We don't take time together for granted – we really value it and focus on it.' Whether engaging with clients or new hires, the business is about relationships, connection and emotions. At the start of a meeting, they will often share how they are feeling:

'so that we all know how we're arriving. And it's culturally something embedded in our fabric, which has meant that the communication of work and the activities is so much easier because we're more in tune with what's going on for us individually… we've educated our people around how to have whole truth conversations.'

Knowing yourself and behaving consistently are the first two steps in building your reputation. The next is your networks.

Work on your networks

Many of the leaders I interviewed reiterated the importance of networks. Sara advises emerging leaders to be curious and expand their networks: 'A network is the most valuable asset that leaders can have. Surround yourself with different and interesting individuals and not all in the same boundary span, so go across different networks.'

Preeti – the CEO of Upshot whom we met in Chapter 3 – says emerging leaders should be proactive: 'Don't wait to win the lottery; buy the ticket. Turn up at networking events. Build your network. Talk to people, even if you don't know anyone in the room.' She also says it's important to remember nobody's out to get you. 'Everybody wants to help you. But you need to go and ask for it. Figure out what it is you want.'

There is a lot of focus on LinkedIn as for networking and brand managers who charge leaders for their LinkedIn brand abound. The power of LinkedIn cannot be ignored. It has nearly one billion members and is the ideal place to connect with future employers and customers. However, it's not the only network out there. We all operate in concentric networks of family, community and society – all of which contain people who can help shine a light on our reputations.

One of the best ways to build a network is to help others, without wanting or asking for anything in return. Being a good person out in the world is the best way to hack the algorithm of the network – if you are also doing good work and talking about it.

Case study: The power of networks

Alayne Oriol Cotterill, who is co-founder and co-CEO of Lion Landscapes, was an outsider in the world of conservation when she first left the UK after her studies. Driven by a passion for animals and Africa, she arrived in Zimbabwe and spent years volunteering, working and building contacts before she was offered her first job.

When Alayne started in conservation it was very male dominated, especially the large carnivore research and capture work that she was doing. After seven years of working in field conservation in Zimbabwe and another ten years in Kenya, Alayne set up the Pride Lion Conservation Alliance with as one of six founding partners. This is an alliance of lion researchers across East Africa, including Kenya, Tanzania, Zambia and Mozambique. The researchers were coincidentally also all women. She says:

> 'Along with five other leaders of lion conservation projects, we started Pride because we were struggling in isolation, trying to be effective leaders on our own, and in competition with others who had the same goal. We thought there must be a better and more collaborative way of working, and that we could have much more impact if we dropped that competitive stance and started really collaborating on a deep level.'

She also says many women in field conservation stop work when they have children, but many of the women in the Pride

Alliance had children and supported each other to keep working. And it's the deep level of support created by the Pride network that Alayne is most proud of. At a time when conservation was competitive and isolated, they showed that 'real collaboration works, and we've been able to scale our conservation efforts using that model.'

Alayne met Amy Dickman, who was running her own lion conservation projects in Tanzania through Oxford University, but it was in Pride that they realized that they had a very similar vision and approach to their conservation work. Amy was doing lion research work in Tanzania, and is now her Lion Landscapes co-CEO. 'Both of us wanted to take the Pride collaboration to another level.' They merged their work in 2020, and Lion Landscapes was born, which they lead as co-CEOs.

While the collaborative approach is better for achieving meaningful conservation impacts in vast landscapes, it's also important for funding:

> 'That's part of the reason why we formed Pride, because we wanted to be big enough to be able to say to donors this is the new model. Pride gave us more influence than we ever had as individual projects and organizations. And that has been influential, because donors often now insist on collaboration, and we hope that the Pride example played a role in the change towards donors insisting on more collaboration.'

There is a hero model in conservation (think of George and Joy Adamson) that is often also white, and Lion Landscapes has pushed back on this by creating a collaborative, ecosystem model that is good for funding, good for teams and good for wildlife.

Alayne and Amy have occasionally been offered individual awards, but they prefer to accept only when the award is shared although this is not always possible. 'There isn't an award for conservation teams, which if you think about it is crazy, so we are going to start our own.'

By creating a supportive network through Pride for themselves and their teams, Alayne and Amy were able to grow a much larger organization, tap into much deeper funding resources and help change the narrative around conservation models. Pride members also offer support to other project leaders beyond Pride, extending the network.

Narratives

Leaders are sometimes threatened by the idea of storytelling. We look at actors and comedians who are brilliant storytellers and think we are under pressure to be like them. Occasionally leaders are natural raconteurs. Others patiently learn the skills. Still others hire executive communicators or consultants like me to help them find and tell the stories. As part of my reputation offering, I ask executives a list of questions to dig out their stories.

The questions fall into three main categories: What are you passionate about? What is your expertise? What makes you credible? There is a fourth category: Who is your audience and who are the people who can tell them about you? This speaks to the network aspect of reputation.

And what's the difference between narrative and story? Most of us use these as synonyms but I found the smartest elaboration in *The Narrative Age*.[4] On the simplest level, stories build narratives and narratives build reputations.

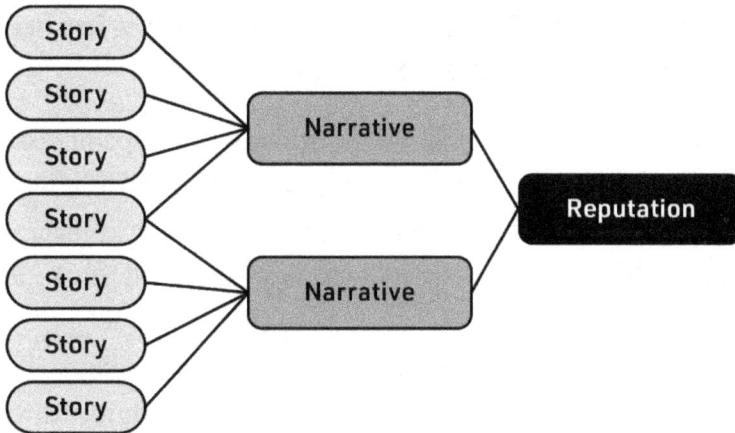

Figure 5: Building your reputation with stories and narratives
Graphic reproduced with permission from Frank Wolf, author of *The Narrative Age*

Frank's research led me to the work of the Narrative Initiative. This is a group of narrative strategists who banded together after the 2016 US election to gain a deeper understanding of how narratives could be put to use to promote racial, social, economic and health equity. They went through several week-long listening campaigns with over 100 narrative and culture change champions in narrative-based social justice work. They identified several clusters in what they call the 'cosmos' of narrative-based work: cognitive and social science, strategic communications, data research and analysis, storytelling, movement building, cultural organizers and narrative strategists.

They think of the relationship between narrative and story as a mosaic:

'What tiles are to mosaics, stories are to narratives. The relationship is symbiotic; stories bring narratives to life by making them relatable and accessible, while narratives infuse stories with deeper meaning.'[5]

Case study: The Springboks – not just a winning story, but a narrative for a nation

The South African national rugby squad – the Springboks – is currently the most the successful rugby team in the world. They've won a record four World Cups, including two back-to-back, and have recently beaten the New Zealand All Blacks four times in a row for the first time since 1949.

This is about so much more than success on the field.

First, during apartheid the rugby team was almost always all-white, and were often banned from playing international matches because of international repulsion at the apartheid system. Then in 1995, the year after the first democratic election that voted Nelson Mandela and the ANC into power, the country hosted the World Cup, played in it for the first time and won – with Mandela in attendance. This is remembered as 'one of the greatest moments in South Africa's sporting history and a watershed moment in the post-apartheid nation building process.'[6]

The Springboks won the World Cup in 2019 and 2023 with a team that represents all populations in the country, led both times by captain Siya Kolisi who overcame poverty to become one of the most recognized rugby players of his generation.

The mixed-race team has devoted fans of all races. The country is united behind them, overcoming differences and inequalities to support the team. South Africa faces its challenges, but the rugby team is a symbol of hope, innovation and what can be achieved when you embrace diversity of all kinds. The team itself is also inspired to play for those at home – their narrative is not 'this one for the team' but 'this one for the country.' Playing for something bigger than themselves inspires them to greater heights.

A recent newspaper article said that 'The Springboks have shown us unity is not about erasing our diversity; it is about recognizing that it can be a source of strength. The Springboks offer a glimpse of what is possible when we set aside the barriers that divide us and work towards a common objective.'[7]

To build your reputation as an individual leader, think through the strategic narratives that make up your reputation, and break down those narratives into stories.

Another great thinker on the topic of strategic narrative is Andy Raskin. While Andy focuses his energy more on the strategic narrative of companies rather than individuals, he helps leadership teams cohere around a single narrative that drives all other parts of the business. For Andy, strategy *is* story.[8]

When it comes to reputation, what you say about yourself and how you say it really matters. Authenticity is critical, and it's hard to be authentic if you haven't done the work to really know and understand yourself. Once you have, you will be aware of how you like to communicate as a leader.

Language

One commonality across nearly all of the interviews with diverse leaders was an awareness of and thoughtfulness about how they use language. It comes down to words.

Vania says that communication is a package. It is not just about the words, but about pairing the communication with the message and confidence. To get to this point, she has worked with communications coaches and her head of communications to reflect on her brand, how she shows up and how she interfaces with staff. 'My big learning is to be open to feedback. Another point is that communication is not about only the how but about the what.' She says leaders must be aware of their style of communication, their brand and how they interact with employees and other audiences.

She doesn't like overly scripted communications. When she writes an update to the organization, she doesn't mind if it is not perfect: 'I like the spontaneity and if it's perfect, then it's not me.'

In terms of her leadership language, Sara also avoids anything overly scripted. She uses unfiltered, emotional language, because 'that is me.' She says her identity gives her freedom to do things differently. She talks about her business as 'limitless' and that gives her space to communicate authentically as a leader but also to grow the business as and how she and the leadership team see fit. Having felt like a fish out of water and not good enough in corporate, she has created a work environment that is creative, open and welcoming.

Antonia also celebrates being authentic in her communication style: 'I'm at the stage now in my leadership journey where I inject as much personality as I have in my private persona into my work persona. And that's also so liberating and so energizing because then you're not working hard at maintaining two personas.'

Don't undermine yourself when you speak. I see an overuse of weasel words that undermine a strongly held opinion. If you have an opinion, own it, don't try to couch it in language such as 'my two cents,' 'personally,' 'in my humble opinion,' or 'for what it's worth.' First, anyone who says they are humble is clearly not, and using words that might seem to soften a blow can often come across as passive aggressive. If you believe something, say it.

David is thoughtful about how they use language, particularly as they operate in a work environment where people come from so many language backgrounds (and this was common across many of the interviews). They try to always understand people's intention. However, it's more nuanced than that:

'So, growing up in an environment where I have been so abused with different words, and I also do get abused every day when I walk on the street, language matters a lot to me. I try to be as empathic as possible, but at the same time to be as assertive as possible. Because empathy will help people have this respect towards each other, and assertiveness will put in the boundaries that are needed.'

As a leader, David tries to communicate in a clear way and has put a lot of effort into improving their English and their business communication. They also try not to be defensive and will always try to sit down with someone and have a conversation to clear the air. They have learned effective communication (talk about the event, talk about your feelings, talk about your need, and then end with the wish) and when asking for feedback, they always ask for examples. Their biggest learning in leadership communication is 'I can acknowledge your feelings, and I acknowledge my feelings, but I do not take responsibility for your feelings.'

Using English as a common language across a global team, means that Antonia also has to be aware of language nuances. She obviates this by being 'Usually very direct: say what you mean and follow through.'

It's that 'follow through' that really matters. Leaders who say things but don't act on them break trust and that is reputational. Your words and your actions must match if you want to build a great reputation as a leader.

Conclusion

Even if you don't have the budget to hire or work with a communicator, the lessons of reputation are still available to you as a leader from an URM. Knowing yourself and how your identity intersects with your leadership style is step one. Understanding and using your networks is step two, and finding your stories and communication style is step three. Be thoughtful and intentional about the language you use, and always ensure that your words and actions meet. Your reputation is at risk if they do not.

From this chapter: Lessons in leadership communication

- Doing good work and talking about it sets you up as an authority as a diverse leader.
- Your record of achievement is a buffer against bias.
- Your network is an algorithm waiting for you to hack.
- Find your stories and tell them.
- Make sure your actions and your words match.

Chapter 11

Reputation equity for founders – when you're both CEO and CCO

One autumn evening, I was sitting at an Afghan restaurant in Ghent with the three co-founders of one of Belgian's leading AI start-ups. One of them asked me, 'What's the difference between marketing and communication?' I was shocked. With my corporate lens, I presumed everyone knew the difference. I stammered something along the lines of marketing is owned media; communication is earned media.

What I was really talking about was reputation – and you can't buy reputation with a marketing budget. You have to earn it. And you earn it, as we have learned, through behaviour, narratives and networks.

Why does reputation matter for diverse founders?

While the statistics on female and Black CEOs in FTSE 100 and Fortune 500 companies are bad, the statistics on funding for female and Black founder CEOs are woeful. It comes down to access, whether it's access to the top jobs or access to funding.

Atomico's very thorough report on the state of European funding in 2024 says that while the bench of European funders has increased, only five percent of Seed funding goes to women today.

While all women teams have doubled the share of pre-Seed funding they receive, there remains a challenge across all other areas of the funding funnel:

> 'All-female teams are less likely to receive further funding than their all-male counterparts. In Europe 47% of women-founded companies secured funding after their first Seed round, compared to 59% of all-male founding teams. As they progress on their capital journey, the gap widens, In fact, by the time they reach their fourth round all-male teams are twice as likely than all-female teams to have secured funding. The same issue is prevalent in the US.'[1]

US statistics are much the same: startups founded exclusively by women raised 2% of the total capital invested in VC-backed start-ups.[2] Black founders received less than 0.5% of US venture capital funding in 2023.[3] In addition, the US is seeing a similar kind of backlash to Black-owned VCs funding diversity-based investments as the backlash to DEI programmes. In July 2024, the Atlanta-based 11th U.S. Circuit Court of Appeals in early June found an anti-affirmative action group's lawsuit that accused Fearless Fund of discrimination would likely succeed, reversing a judge's decision to allow the firm to continue making grants while the case proceeded.[4]

Worldwide, the picture is similar: only 1.5% of funds raised by African startups were allocated to women,[5] while in Asia Pacific women make up only 6% of startup founders.[6]

Building a reputation for diverse founders is absolutely critical in terms of getting funding. While I am not saying that those who haven't received funding are failing in some way – because it's more than that; it's systemic – I am saying that being a known quantity helps. Yekaterina Kovaleva and a group of researchers from LUT

University in Finland looked at all the factors preventing women from entering entrepreneurship, and found that most of the success stories we read and see are about male entrepreneurs.[7] We need to see the narratives of female entrepreneurs.

Several factors come into play for diverse founders when trying to raise money. You need a clear narrative about both your company and yourself. Your story matters. The power of networks comes into play here too – when researching a venture capitalist before a meeting, spend some time on LinkedIn. Work out who they're connected to so that you are connected as well. Find a way to demonstrate to them that people in their network whom they trust, know and trust you.

One of the VCs I know very well (I am married to him), always asks start-up founders 'What do you believe that no-one else believes?' By asking that question, he's not trying to uncover any contrarian positions; he's looking for a strong belief – one that is so strong that it's going to carry you from pre-seed all the way to becoming a unicorn and preferably an eventual initial public offering (IPO). He wants to see a big belief that will build a big company. Your strong belief is based on your story and the story of your business. Make it unique, strong and credible.

Speaking to that strong belief, startup advisor and former CEO, Dave Kellogg, also points out that while CEOs think in quarters, founders should think in years or even eras. He talks about speaking of your startup in terms of belief-driven eras:

'I often say that strategy is best analyzed in reflection. Meaning that somehow everything is clearer and simpler when you look back ten or 20 years to reflect upon what happened. In fact, I often encourage people to do a future look-back when formulating strategy: "imagine it's ten years from now and your company won in the market – now tell me why."'[8]

Communicating as a founder CEO

As a founder, particularly in the early stages, as well as being the CEO, you are the reputation manager and the CCO of your business. The company story is your story – the two are intertwined.

Think of Musema Robert, whose story we first saw in Chapter 3. He was raised by his single mother, who worked hard to ensure he got the education he needed. His Ugandan fashion brand Msema Culture grew out of his love of fashion, his adherence to Rasta culture and his passion to help women rise out of poverty. He has released at least one range of clothing inspired by menstrual equity. His brand story is his story. When he talks about himself, he's talking about his brand. The two are enmeshed.

We also met Katja Kolmetz in Chapter 3. As CEO and founder of Wavemakers, Katja's mission to redefine leadership is now embodied in the Wavemakers programme for over 15,000 emerging leaders. It grew out of her frustration in corporate, where she was often the only woman and the youngest person in the room. Since she had studied communications and not computer science, she always felt like an outlier. 'I never felt empowered as a leader. I've always tried to fit into the expectations that my managers had for me, or how I saw other leaders. And even if I was successful and would get positive feedback, it didn't make me happy.'

Katja now works to empower leaders who do not fit the current stereotype of leadership and to find leadership inside themselves. Her story is the story of the business.

Another mission-driven founder is Katarzyna Koba (preferred name 'Koba'), CEO and founder of RoboKoba and proprietary owner of the SensiVR Health technology, who has been recognized as one of Poland's top 100 women in AI. Koba identifies as a female leader, a digital artist and being a neurodiverse person. Her passion at school and university was new media.

As a digital artist, Koba was inspired by neuro-artists who conduct research into their own emotional reactions to multisensory environments. They collect their biometric data while experimenting with an over-stimulated sensory environment, using strobe lights or ultrasound to prove that specific areas of the brain are activated by technological impact. Koba believes that this is very promising for healthcare and technology. Her start-up SensiVR Health is aimed at providing digital therapy for children with sensory processing issues, including neurodevelopment disorders, using a virtual sensory room for children that engages all the senses and helps them overcome learning difficulties.

Koba translates her passion for new media – and her deep empathy for children with neurological disorders – into her business. Her story and the story of her business are one. And her belief in it is big, so big that after finishing university with little money and even less English she moved to Brighton, UK, for two years to build a network with the neuro-artists whose work she admired. She did this successfully and moved home to Poland with new conviction that she was on the right track to build a breakthrough business.

This close matching of founder to story in the early stages of a business means founders are narrative driven. They are their own CCO and they need to learn to tell their story really well, and become strong communicators, in order to attract investors and raise the profile of their businesses.

How later-stage founders communicate

We've already met founders Tony Jamous, Sara Daw and Porter Braswell. At the time of writing, Tony has 80,000 followers on LinkedIn where he writes on the topics of remote work and conscious leadership. Sara has 5,000 followers and is rapidly making a name for herself on the topic of C-Suite as Service with the 2024 publication of her book *Strategy and Leadership as Service*. This has been accompanied by several top-tier media articles and podcast appearances that have positioned her as a thought leader on the topic. Porter has 115,000 followers, a regular *Fast Company* column, a HBR podcast and a book – all focusing on the topic of increasing diversity in leadership.

All three are acknowledged thought leaders in the spaces they have carved out for themselves, and their thought leadership is driven by personal passion that matches their business story. They have become authorities, based on doing the work and talking about it. Authority combined with business success creates new reputational equity for leaders with diverse identities.

Porter says: 'I now realize that my difference and the lack of people who look like me doing the work that I'm doing is actually a huge asset. I can go into a company and speak with authority around the experience of being a person of colour in this country.'

When he was building Jopwell, he was fighting with investors to get them to understand that diversity recruiting matters. Now, having successfully sold Jopwell and built two new companies, as well as being an investor himself, the conversation has changed:

> 'You know what? I know something you don't know. And you're supposed to be paid to know everything. Well, you don't know this. So now the leverage completely flipped in like investor dialogues, because I was the expert educating somebody who was supposed to be an expert on everything about a thing they had no idea about. My evolution has been one-off and it's not something that holds me back. It's a thing that is a competitive advantage for me.'

Building authority to this scale is time-consuming, but with all three it is driven by the passion for their subject matter, business success and a clear-eyed acknowledgement that being an authority promotes their business. Building authority drives reputation equity.

Authority building

Not every founder or C-Suite start-up executive has the bandwidth to write books, but there are ways to build authority (and hence reputation) with the same passion as Sara, Porter and Tony.

Emma Sinclair is the CEO of EnterpriseAlumni, an alumni management software company that she founded with her brother. Being entrepreneurs is written in their genes: their father is real estate entrepreneur Neil Sinclair. At 29, Emma became the youngest person in the world to have floated a company, doing so on the London Stock Exchange. In 2014, she was appointed UNICEFs first business ambassador, conceiving their first ever crowdfund to roll out Innovation Labs in refugee camps. And in 2016, she was awarded an MBE by the Queen for Services to Entrepreneurship.

Emma is a thought leader and frequently pens articles for *The Guardian* and *The Telegraph*. She's built her reputation by being a brilliant entrepreneur but also via her advocacy. In 2022, she led the UK initiative of more than 200 large companies to scale up RefuAid, a charity who fund full-time English lessons and cover exam and recertification costs for skilled refugees so that they can find commensurate work, in the light of the Ukraine war.[9] She's also a vocal advocate for improving funding to women-led companies, and when the latest dire statistics were released in 2023, Emma started the grassroots #BeMyAngel campaign to encourage members of the public who were equally horrified to invest directly in the companies led by female founders and be part of the solution.[10]

With 15,000 followers on LinkedIn and 25,000 on X, she has an impressive network, but for Emma it's more about personal networks. She once advised me to 'remember to pay it back – it's not just about what you can get out of your network. It's about what you can do for them.'

Doing things for people is a key part of advocacy, but it's also a great way to activate a network and build a reputation for being a good person. Emma says: 'When I do ask for help, and I'm usually asking on behalf of others, people know what I stand for and step up magnificently. Do nice things for others and others may be inspired to do the same.'

Another example is Zoe Colosimo, COO and founding member of Neighbourly in the UK. Neighbourly is a certified B Corp that helps businesses make a positive impact in their communities through volunteering, local fundraising, grants and surplus product redistribution – all in one platform. With funding cuts in social services, a cost-of-living crisis and environmental imperatives, the Neighbourly platform helps businesses give away resources to support the communities they serve – importantly, enabling supermarkets to redistribute surplus food by matching them to charities and food banks in their areas – and recently reached the milestone of donating 200 million meals.[11]

Zoe, whose team has built the platform from the ground up with a network of 40,000 local charities, describes it:

> 'You've got two entities – on one side, businesses that have something to give; on the other side, you have community causes that need something, and an algorithm in the middle matches those two things together, making it possible to deliver localized impact at scale. Importantly, you can automatically measure the value of those transactions going through the platform and report with great accuracy the positive impact being generated through each contribution.'

Zoe's authority and motivation stems from the belief that complex challenges must be addressed and not avoided just because they are difficult. Building a technical platform that works, scales and creates impact in communities whilst reducing environmental footprint and allowing businesses to report on that impact as part of environmental, social and governance (ESG), corporate social responsibility

(CSR) and marketing initiatives has not been simple, but it is the ultimate marketplace for sustainable communities. Neighbourly is consistently winning awards and garnering press headlines in the UK, and Zoe is frequently invited as a public speaker.

Kate Bradley is the CEO and co-founder of Lately.AI. Formerly a DJ on satellite radio station Sirius/XM which broadcast to 20 million listeners a day, Kate started Lately in 2014 based on her understanding of how to turn listeners into fans and customers into evangelists. Lately scripts social media messaging using their about-to-be patented Neuroscience-Driven AI™, and predicts which messages will convert into sales. She says, 'I knew that when the mind engages it has to access nostalgia and memory and emotion, and all those components must be in place in order for trust to happen. And when you have trust and the consumer is buying, that's how you have that pathway to evangelism.'

Lately was building proprietary language models long before the AI hype.

When Kate talks about reputation she says: 'you don't need to be the light in the room. Be the magnet that makes other people be the light. When you do that, it's much more powerful and beneficial. You're memorable when you lift other people up, and they walk away thinking, "Oh I have a connection there."'

Kate invests time in talking about her business: 'I do a lot of podcasts, a lot of interviews, a lot of writing, a lot of earned media. I think it's really important.' Having listened to some of these podcasts and read her interviews, it's clear to me that what Kate is doing is effective telling.

How founders and startup CEOs manage reputation

As we've seen, early-stage founders are narrative and mission-driven. They are their story. However, as the business grows, they have to start making hiring decisions and ceding some of the reputation management to others. The first brand-related hire a start-up makes is a head of marketing. This makes complete sense, since they want to create a sales funnel. And very quickly, with all the things they have to build and manage, the head of marketing finds the budget to hire someone to do PR. However, PR only looks after one audience – the media – and as companies grow, and founder CEOs have too much on their plates, they need to hire in more communicators to look after the others.

I've seen an interesting decision-making process by founders in Paris, who, despite the strong French culture, decide to make English the language of the business because their ambition is global. And if founders are hiring too much from their own culture, they should be aware that they risk a homogenous point of view which can be counterproductive if they're looking to build a global company.

Kim Scott says that startups often 'begin with a culture where people challenge each other directly and even fiercely, but also show that they care fiercely. However, as the business grows and new people join the firm, it's impossible to know everyone's name, let alone to have strong relationships with everyone.'[12]

It's at this point, I'd advise a startup to hire in communications, either full-time or a consultant.

When do startups actively need communications advice?

Location

In the early stage, founders can usually communicate by walking around. Once they expand to more than one location, suddenly they're communicating by email, Slack and in online meetings. This is a shift that means a new tone and new communications awareness. I advise clients that this is the time to make the first internal communications hire – someone who can help the founder keep message coherence between different locations and also possibly different cultures.

Employees are an important audience, with a direct line to the outside world in the form of social media, and founders need to keep all employees engaged and aligned no matter where they're located.

Layoffs

Investors might advise a reduction in force (RIF). Worky CEO Maya talked in Chapter 6 about the challenge of getting the organizational culture back on track and everyone working in the same direction after a layoff. Having an internal communicator or communications consultant will help you manage a RIF in a humane and empathetic way – and help you to remember all your audiences to avoid reputational risk.

Change of CEO

As we've seen, the founder embodies the company narrative. When the founder leaves and a new CEO comes on board, it's essential that the new leader attaches to the narrative in a way that is authentic and real for them. A new person brings new stories, experiences and skills, and a talented communicator will help the new CEO match these to the business.

Conclusion

Founders who've hired communicators and say they don't know what their communicators are doing should also look to themselves: it means you're not engaging with them enough and ensuring that all the communications activities are strategy and business driven. It's also a wasted opportunity – reputation is the water in which your communicators swim and they could be building yours towards the next great investment opportunity. According to Sifted, the most-followed founder CEOs on LinkedIn raise 20% more cash than their less-followed counterparts.[13]

Founder CEOs are building a plane while flying it, while corporate CEOs tend to inherit an already completed plane that might need some innovation to beat competitors. Diverse founders have the additional challenge that it is harder to secure the investment they need to grow their business. Using the tenets of reputation – behaviour, networks and narratives – they can become strong communicators, develop a profile for themselves and their business, and be seen by all audiences as an authority with a big era-defining business idea.

From this chapter: Lessons in leadership communication

- For founders, personal story and company story are intertwined in one narrative.
- As startups become scale-ups, founders need to build authority.
- Think of this as the thing you believe that no-one else believes that will help you build an era-defining business.
- When your company grows beyond one location, it's time to hire in communication expertise.
- Spend time with your communicators – they will help you build authority, be seen as the leader you are and help your business grow its reputation with all audiences including those all-important investors.

Chapter 12

Towards new leaders

The tagline of this book is 'mastering reputation management to reshape the C-Suite' and as we've seen progress to get women and people from URM into the C-Suite is slow. So far, we've looked at how people from diverse backgrounds can and do use reputation management, or effective telling, to enhance their leadership and how they can rely on a reputation manager or communicator to help them improve these skills.

Changing the C-Suite is multi-directional: we need to get new leaders around the boardroom table to innovate our organizations from within and new leaders need to show up with their value externalized ready to take the step.

Not everyone can be CEO. It's a zero-sum game.[1] Not everyone who wants to will make it to the C-Suite. However, externalizing your value, having a superb record of achievement, doing the work and talking about it will help your chances.

Trust in politics and the media has dwindled to such an extent that people now look to business as the most trusted institution. Social media has eroded the corporate boundaries so that bad leadership behaviour is no longer protected by a wall of silence. Trust is lost when companies try to explain the gap between their values and their behaviour. The bedrock of our workplace culture is still paternalistic, autocratic and short termist.

However, transformational leadership does exist. Command and control no longer works, as the CEOs who are trying to mandate post-pandemic returns to office are seeing. You might get people's bodies in their seats, but you might have lost them emotionally. Let's take a look at a transformational leader.

Case study: Leadership change comes from within

Tony Jamous is the founder of the unicorn Oyster (a unicorn is a start-up whose value exceeds $1 billion). We learned earlier in the book that Tony incorporated Oyster shortly before the pandemic based on the convictions that employees all over the world deserve fair and equitable opportunities no matter where they live and that the world is ready for conscious leadership.

Tony grew up in war-torn Lebanon where he 'saw things no child should see' and he learned that 'we could not trust men in this world.' His family fled to France where Tony went to university and began work.

At Oyster, Tony practices business karma. This is the idea that if you put your effort where your heart is, the universe will help you succeed.

Referring to the world's failure to achieve the 2030 UN Sustainable Development Goals, Tony says 'we are not in a sustainability crisis; we are in a consciousness crisis.'

His thesis is that leaders have to change themselves first before making a positive impact in the world. For Tony, leaders need to manage their emotions and their responses to fear and become non-reactive. His goal is to lead without ego, and to create a mission-inspired organization. He says Oyster is hyper-diverse, with 50% gender diversity on the management team and the board, and 100% remote.

At Oyster, 'everyone is invited to be their true self. You have to create the psychological safety so people are not afraid to show up as their true self. And I create psychological safety by being non-reactive to bad news, by defaulting to trust and defaulting to assuming best intent.'

Tony says self-expression is therapy for him. He has built a following of over 80,000 on LinkedIn where he talks about running a business that is 100% remote and about conscious leadership. His purpose is modelling conscious, and more humane, leadership for other leaders. 'There's more to work than hitting a quarterly profit number, right, and if I can help some leaders to see that, then that would be aligned with my purpose right now.'

He believes that if leaders could unlock the mental armour that causes fear, and hurts others and themselves, then they would be happier, more fulfilled, balanced and healthy.

If leaders can unlock the mental armour that causes fear and hurts others, their employees and organizations would be happier and healthier too. And if this feels like emotional labour, that's because it is. Kim Scott says that emotional labour is not just part of the job, but key to being a good boss.[2]

New leaders are doing the emotional labour. As Peter Figge described, and as many others showed, because of their identities they done the labour and now know how to be conscious and humane leaders for others. Transformational leaders transform themselves first.

Psychologist Esther Perel says we used to go to work to make a living, but now we go to work to make meaning.[3] Workplaces need to create meaningful conversations around diversity and identity so that we start to see people who are different from the current workplace leadership norm as leaders in the making.

According to McKinsey, in an analysis of academic literature and a global survey of nearly 200,000 people in 81 organizations, there are four types of behaviours that account for 89% of leadership effectiveness: being supportive, operating with a strong orientation toward results, seeking different perspectives and solving problems effectively.[4] This starts with self-knowledge, which McKinsey calls inside-out leadership.[5]

Inside-out leadership

The leaders I've interviewed have a strong focus on self-knowledge and understanding as the foundation of their leadership skills. They are intensely aware of language and how they use it, and they are highly conscious of how the language they use lands with their audiences. They are conscious of perception, which is critical as reputation is two-way.

They are aware that everything they say and do makes meaning for the people they lead. Porter showed us how he learned that as a CEO he did not have to be unapproachable and intimidating. By changing his leadership behaviour, he changed the behaviour of those around him. We saw that leaders need to be very clear on whether they are articulating an idea, a closely held belief or an instruction, since people will act based on their words.

Inclusive leaders

Inclusive language is not a one-off lesson. You will have to keep learning, so don't be hard on yourself or those who give you feedback. And if you have committed a micro-aggression, and someone takes you aside quietly to give you feedback, accept that in the spirit from which it comes. If you wish to advise someone that their words or behaviour have been insensitive, have a private and constructive conversation based on learning not shaming.

Make space in the workplace for difficult or previously taboo topics, such as race, gender, menopause, neurodiversity, childcare, elder care, sexual and gender identity, mental health and unseen perceived disabilities such as hearing loss. This helps lighten the load that people from diverse identities carry and makes it easier to recognize leadership in them. Conversations are infinitely more effective than campaigns.

Inclusive leadership behaviours, as Priya Bates and Advita Patel show, include asking powerful questions, being curious and asking for regular feedback, challenging poor behaviours and practices (we saw both Mona and Kholi do this), creating safe spaces for colleagues to speak up (and this means not allowing loud voices to dominate conversation), and being aware of your assumptions and biases.

Inclusivity also means being thoughtful about the language you use.

Redefining leadership

The patterns of what we see or usually expect of leaders are being broken by emerging leaders. They are redefining what leadership means for themselves, and they are not asking for permission for how they show up in the workplace. Emerging leaders are highly aware that representation matters, but they know that as individuals they get to choose when and how they articulate their identity or diverse background. They know that speaking to their identity gives them an edge, but they do not accept the othering that happens when people ask them to speak for a demographic. Emerging leaders are skipping the traditional hierarchy, following non-linear careers and building work based on passion. They say leadership is as much about being perceived as a leader by others as it is about having a management position.

From more senior leaders, we saw that those who value learning rather than the next step on the management rung can make the biggest leaps. They also see that there is no point in being palatable or following a leadership archetype; instead, they find joy in showing up as themselves. While the idea of authenticity seems contested, it is only so when it is performed. It must come from a genuine place, tied to personal values. New leaders know they need to be double-loop learners who understand a problem as something to be fixed as well as something to learn from, and they create the culture they want to see in their own teams.

New leaders know the power of being themselves. As Kholi says if you emulate someone's leadership style you lose your identity and then you can't be effective. 'If you can bring your uniqueness to the boardroom, you effect change.'

A critical part of leadership is building a reputation.

Reputation is also inside-out

You build your reputation from the inside, starting with your values. It is a long game, and you can't control every aspect of it, but you can build a narrative moat as your competitive advantage. You also need to think about your behaviour and your network. Trust fails when your words and your behaviours don't match – this goes back to authenticity. In leadership, vulnerability is strength.

People are more likely to follow you if you are vulnerable about how you feel. Your vulnerability can help others feel safe, and this encourages the diversity of opinions needed for innovation. This is not about being nice or likable; it's about being honest and creating the diversity and conflict necessary for innovation (Linda Hill's creative abrasion).

Your reputation is portable, and if you talk about your achievements and your record of success, this can get you to the next leadership role. Doing good work and talking about it sets you up as an authority. Your record of achievement is a buffer against bias, and your network is a powerful algorithm waiting for you to hack. Link your work successes and achievements to strategy: this demonstrates not only that you understand it but also that you know how to move it forward. This alone makes you a leader.

Social media is part of every leader's reputation toolbox. It cannot be ignored. However, social media is also where crisis can hit. You need to have crisis protocols in place and when a crisis arrives, do not panic. Listen to your communicators: they know what to do, when and in what order. Give them the trust they deserve.

Lean on your communicators

Find the communications support you need to build a personal narrative moat against personal crisis, as well as a company narrative moat. As a CEO from an URM not doing both is risky and a wasted opportunity, because, having bested the glass ceiling, you now face the glass cliff. Work with your CCO or head of communications to ensure that your reputation is portable, and this will protect your career longevity.

Remember your CCO is the only member of your leadership team solely devoted to protecting both your and your company's reputation. By building a relationship of trust, you give the CCO the mandate to own both your and your company's reputation. Build a reputation strategy with your CCO or executive communicator, revisit it every quarter and don't be afraid to take risks and experiment. Remember to recognize and thank your CCO or head of communication for their unseen labour in service of your and the company's reputation.

For founders, personal story and company story are usually intertwined in a single narrative. However, as startups become scale-ups, communication and storytelling needs to focus on a variety of different audiences. Founders need to build authority to be seen as the leader of an era-defining business. Be aware of when you need to hire in communications expertise and above all, spend time with your communicators. They will help you build authority, be seen as the leader you are and help your business grow its reputation with all your allies and audiences (including investors).

The aspects of reputation that we first saw in Chapter 1 and which have been threaded throughout the book – your character and competence, as well as your ability to create coherence in the context we live in – are equally key to your ability to lead.

Character and coherence are not enough; neither are character and competence. All three aspects of leadership must be fulfilled otherwise trust is missing. And the new leaders we need have all three. There is no incongruence between their reputations and how they lead.

And this comes down to authenticity – if your inner values (all the work you've done on self-understanding and transformation, and which form your character) match how you behave (your competence) you will create coherence for others who will believe that you're authentic. If there's a mismatch, people read you as inauthentic, which is devastating for your reputation, and breaks trust.

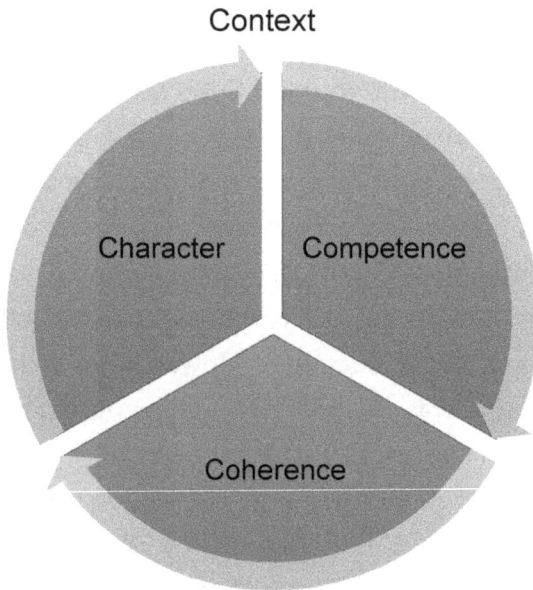

Figure 6: Reputation and authenticity match

Conclusion

Reputation differs from personal brand in that it is about perception. And, as we've seen, leaders from diverse backgrounds are hyper-aware of perception and for this reason are thoughtful about the language they use and how their words land. How you are seen is as important as what you say.

This deep awareness means that leaders from diverse backgrounds don't see leadership – or reputation – as an artefact, or a rung on the management ladder. Both are living processes that they must constantly tend and nurture through character, competence and creating coherence.

We need new leaders to lead us into the future of work. Many of the problems we face in the world and the workplace are systemic, but leaders from diverse backgrounds or of diverse identities can take heart. You have done the work. You have understood and changed yourselves where necessary. You know how to lead in a humane way, that is congruent with your values and the people who you lead. You are the leaders we need in this moment.

Acknowledgements

Attempting to chart the intersection between leadership, diversity and reputation was not something I could manage alone.

I am grateful to my professors, tutors, teachers and cohort in the Change Leadership programme at HEC Paris and Oxford Saïd Business School – you set a course without which this book would not have been conceived.

Heartfelt thanks go to all of the nearly 60 interviewees, not all of whom are directly quoted but all of whom helped me – with their kindness, insights and time – start to outline the map. My beta readers sharpened its contours. Thank you for your feedback and ideas.

I have so much appreciation for Alison Jones and her entire team at Practical Inspiration Publishing who helped me navigate every step of the publishing voyage. Small but perfectly formed, they are expert and highly professional and helped me feel guided and coached.

My very dear family and friends are both near and far. Wherever you are in the world, whether in port cities or inland, your love and enthusiastic support spurred me onwards.

My nearest and dearest – Thomas, Lily, Daisy and Ollie – are my guiding stars, my daily joy and inspiration. Thank you for being you.

Resources

Checklist 1

This checklist organizes the key considerations for hiring or applying for a Chief Communications Officer (CCO) role from the perspectives of the CEO, CHRO, and the CCO themselves.

CEO checklist:

- ☐ Is this person competent enough to handle the basics of the CCO role?
- ☐ Does their experience demonstrate they understand what the job entails?
- ☐ Do they have the self-awareness to admit what they do not know?
- ☐ Do they demonstrate willingness to learn and adapt?
- ☐ Is this a person I want at my side during a crisis?
- ☐ Do I want to spend time with them?
- ☐ Would I trust their advice?
- ☐ Do they understand the difference between working for me and working for the company?
- ☐ Should this person report to me?
- ☐ Is there a place for them on the leadership team?
- ☐ How will I make time and space for them?
- ☐ Do we need to be co-located?
- ☐ If we are not co-located, how will I ensure we get enough time and space together?
- ☐ What are the guidelines around texting?
- ☐ How will I encourage authentic feedback?
- ☐ How will I respond if this person brings me bad news?

CHRO checklist:

- ☐ Which reporting line makes the most sense for protecting company reputation?
- ☐ Should this individual sit on the leadership team?
- ☐ Do they have the skills and experience to manage the role?
- ☐ Do they have the character and courage to give the CEO honest feedback?
- ☐ Will they be able to deliver bad news?
- ☐ Would I want this person at my side if we have an employee-generated crisis?

CCO checklist:

- ☐ What is the reporting line?
- ☐ If reporting to the CEO, is there a role on the leadership team?
- ☐ If not reporting to the CEO, how do I manage the interlocutor?
- ☐ If not reporting to the CEO, do I want this job?
- ☐ How do I get clarity on time and space with the CEO?
- ☐ How do I get clarity on time and space with the CEO?
- ☐ How does the CEO like to be communicated with in non-crisis times?
- ☐ How does the CEO like to be communicated with in crisis times?
- ☐ What are the guidelines around texting?
- ☐ Is there space for authentic feedback?
- ☐ Does the CEO understand that my loyalty is to the company first, and to the CEO second?
- ☐ What is the current reputation situation (managing, mitigating, crisis, or repair)?
- ☐ Who are the audiences, and what are they saying?

Checklist 2

Questions for the CEO and the Chief Communications Officer (CCO) to evaluate when the CCO is already in the role. This checklist helps both the CEO and CCO to continuously assess and improve their working relationship, ensuring that they remain aligned, especially during crises or high-pressure situations.

CEO checklist:

- ☐ Is this relationship working?
- ☐ Are we best placed to manage reputational risk when it hits?
- ☐ Do I need to adjust time and space fulfilments to ensure we are building trust?
- ☐ Do we need more formal or informal time together?
- ☐ How can I give the CCO the most time and space with the least amount of effort?
- ☐ Should they be on the leadership team?
- ☐ If not, should they have access to leadership team (LT) meetings?
- ☐ Do I trust them and their advice?
- ☐ Have we built enough trust to manage a reputational crisis together?
- ☐ Do I still want them at my side if there is a crisis?
- ☐ Do they put the company before me?
- ☐ Are we too close for the CCO to remain unbiased?

CCO checklist:

- ☐ Is this relationship working?
- ☐ What changes do I need to request to improve it?
- ☐ Do I understand the CEO's working style?
- ☐ Do I know how the CEO prefers to work when a crisis hits?

☐ Do I feel comfortable giving genuine advice and feedback?
☐ Does the CEO understand that I need to always put the company first?
☐ Are we too close for me to remain unbiased?

Notes

Introduction

[1] www.mckinsey.com/mhi/our-insights/reframing-employee-health-moving-beyond-burnout-to-holistic-health

[2] www.youtube.com/watch?v=zeAEFEXvcBg

[3] www.edelman.com/trust/2023/trust-barometer

Chapter 1: The leadership crisis

[1] Tomas Chamorro-Premuzic, *Why Do So Many Incompetent Men Become Leaders?* (Harvard Business Review, 2019), p. 6.

[2] ibid, p. 42.

[3] Mary Ann Sieghart, *The Authority Gap* (Penguin Random House, 2021), p. 16.

[4] Gareth Morgan, *Images of Organization* (Sage, 2006).

[5] ibid, p. 219.

[6] ibid, p. 6.

[7] www.indeed.com/lead/the-great-disconnect-what-job-seekers-want-vs-what-employers-offer?hl=en

[8] John Kay, *The Corporation in the 21st Century* (Profile Books, 2024), p. 30.

[9] ibid, p. 238.

[10] www.forbes.com/sites/annesugar/2022/12/15/what-to-do-about-burnout-jennifer-moss-shares-insights-from-her-book-the-burnout-epidemic/

[11] Zhong, et al. Workplace aggression and employee performance: A meta-analytic investigation of mediating mechanisms and cultural contingencies. *Journal of Applied Psychology*, 3 October, 2024.

[12] Kim Scott, *Radical Candor* (Pan Macmillan, 2017), p. xi.

[13] Bernard Bass, From transactional to transformational leadership: Learning to share the vision. *Organizational Dynamics*, Winter, 90, 1990.

[14]　Lauren Eaton, Todd Bridgmann and Stephen Cummings, Advancing the democratization of work: A new intellectual history of transformational leadership theory. *Leadership*, 20(3), 125–43, 2024.

[15]　www.edelman.com/trust/2022-trust-barometer

[16]　www.edelman.com/trust/2023-trust-barometer

[17]　www.edelman.com/trust/2024-trust-barometer

[18]　www.linkedin.com/posts/martinboehringer_communication-is-powerful-now-its-getting-activity-6902609278230700032-8o8E?utm_source=share&utm_medium=member_desktop

[19]　www.washingtonpost.com/business/2022/03/08/russia-company-boycott-yale-list/

[20]　David Waller and Rupert Younger, *The Reputation Game* (OneWorld, 2017), p. 181.

[21]　https://edition.cnn.com/videos/business/2024/01/22/kyte-baby-ceo-issues-apologies-bernal-cnntm-vpx.cnn

Chapter 2: Diversity still matters

[1]　www.cnbc.com/video/2023/01/21/340-billion-pledged-to-racial-equity-after-george-floyd-mckinsey.html#:~:text=Nearly%20three%20years%20after%20George,companies%20to%20support%20racial%20equity

[2]　https://nypost.com/2024/07/17/business/microsoft-fires-dei-team-becoming-latest-company-to-ditch-woke-policy-report/

[3]　https://fortune.com/2024/06/04/share-of-fortune-500-businesses-run-by-women/

[4]　https://fortune.com/2024/02/09/black-ceos-fortune-500-high-workplace-diversity/

[5]　https://ftsewomenleaders.com/wp-content/uploads/2024/04/ftse-women-leaders-report-final-april-2024.pdf

[6]　https://fortune.com/europe/2024/03/08/international-womens-day-iwd-leading-europes-biggest-companies-success-has-no-limit/

[7]　https://parkerreview.co.uk/wp-content/uploads/2024/03/The-Parker-Review-March-2024.pdf

[8]　www.fastcompany.com/91137051/what-is-the-future-of-dei-2

[9]　www.fastcompany.com/91137051/what-is-the-future-of-dei-2

[10]　www.ted.com/talks/ray_dalio_how_to_build_a_company_where_the_best_ideas_win/transcript?subtitle=en

[11] Porter Braswell, *Let Them See You* (Lorena Jones Books, 2017), p. 113.

[12] ibid, p. 112.

[13] Priya Bates and Advita Patel, *Building Inclusive Cultures* (Kogan Page, 2023), p. 126.

[14] ibid, p. 286.

[15] www.bbc.com/worklife/article/20210730-the-coded-language-that-holds-women-back-at-work

Chapter 3: Finding the leader within – landing or creating a dream job

[1] Porter Braswell, *Let Them See You* (Lorena Jones Books, 2017), p. 86.

Chapter 4: Finding the right culture – keeping a dream job

[1] Jeffrey Pfeffer, *Power* (Harvard Business Press, 2010), p. 161.

Chapter 5: Understanding reputation

[1] Charles Fombrun, *Reputation: Realizing Value from the Corporate Image* (HBS Press, 1996), Introduction.

[2] ibid, p. 18.

[3] Robert Eccles, Scott Newquist and Roland Schatz, *Reputation and Its Risks* (Harvard Business Review, 2007), www.researchgate.net/profile/Roland-Schatz-2/publication/6460600_Reputation_and_its_risks/links/56b2497c08ae5ec4ed4b3660/Reputation-and-its-risks.pdf

[4] ibid, p. 22.

[5] Danuta Szwajca, Dilemmas of reputation risk management: Theoretical study. *Corporate Reputation Review*, 21, p. 166, 2018.

[6] https://blog.reputationx.com/corporate-reputation-guide

[7] David Waller and Rupert Younger, *The Reputation Game* (OneWorld, 2017), p. xv.

[8] Frank Wolf, *The Narrative Age* (self published, 2024), p. 27.

[9] ibid, p. 129.

[10] ibid, p. 144.

¹¹ Charles Fombrun, *Reputation: Realizing Value from the Corporate Image* (HBS Press, 1996), p. 68.

¹² Rachel Botsman, *Who Can You Trust: How Technology Brought Us Together and Why It Might Drive Us Apart* (Public Affairs, 2017), p. 144.

¹³ John Blakey (n.d.), https://trustedexecutive.com/nine-habits-of-trust/resources-overview/

¹⁴ Rachel Botsman, *Who Can You Trust: How Technology Brought Us Together and Why It Might Drive Us Apart* (Public Affairs, 2017), p. 123.

Chapter 6: Understanding corporate versus CEO reputation

¹ Hurst, 2023. https://fortune.com/europe/2023/09/15/bp-ceo-exit-chaos/

² Strasberg, 2023. www.reuters.com/business/energy/bp-ceo-bernard-looney-resign-ft-2023-09-12/

³ AFP, 2023. www.barrons.com/news/bp-shares-sink-after-ceo-quits-over-relationships-6011ca88

⁴ P. Clarke, 2023. www.fnlondon.com/articles/citigroups-dealmaking-fees-jump-34-in-third-quarter-but-ma-still-lags-20231013

⁵ Reuters, 2023. www.reuters.com/business/finance/citigroups-business-heads-revamped-structure-2023-09-13/#:~:text=Sept%2013%20(Reuters)%20%2D%20Citigroup,its%20profit%20and%20share%20price

⁶ English, 2023. www.barrons.com/articles/citigroup-banks-fraser-4be843f3

⁷ David Waller and Rupert Younger, *The Reputation Game* (OneWorld, 2017), p. 17.

⁸ Charles O'Reilly and Michael Tushman, *Lead and Disrupt: How to Solve the Innovator's Dilemma* (Stanford Business Books, 2016), p. 10.

⁹ Chris Ansell, Arjen Boin and Moshe Farjoun. Dynamic conservatism: How institutions change to remain the same. *Research in the Sociology of Organizations*, 44, 89–119, 2020. https://doi.org/10.1108/S0733-558X20150000044005

¹⁰ David Waller and Rupert Younger, *The Reputation Game* (OneWorld, 2017), p. 226.

¹¹ Geoffrey Love and Michael Bednar. The face of the firm: The influence of CEOs on corporate reputation. *Academy of Management Journal*, 60(4), 1466, 2017.

¹² David Waller and Rupert Younger, *The Reputation Game* (OneWorld, 2017), p. 231.

13 https://en.wikipedia.org/wiki/Timeline_of_social_media

14 https://modelthinkers.com/mental-model/surface-area-of-luck

15 Jeffrey Pfeffer, *Power* (Harper Business, 2010), p. 148.

Chapter 7: Reputational risk and crisis management

1   Danuta Szwajca. Dilemmas of reputation risk management: Theoretical study. *Corporate Reputation Review*, 21(4), 165–78, 2018. https://doi.org/10.1057/s41299-018-0052-9

2   Dominik Heil. Reputation Risk. In Robert Heath and Winni Johansen (eds) *The International Encyclopedia of Strategic Communication* (pp. 1–6). Wiley, 2018. https://doi.org/10.1002/9781119010722.iesc0150

3   Robert Eccles, Scott Newquist and Roland Schatz. *Reputation and Its Risks* (Harvard Business Review, 2007). https://hbr.org/2007/02/reputation-and-its-risks

4   Barry Mitnick, John Mahon and Richard McGowan. Reputation-sets. *Journal of Public Affairs*, 20(1), 2020. https://doi.org/10.1002/pa.2062

5   Rajeev Syal. *Sue Gray: Who is official tasked with investigating No 10 party claims?* The Guardian, 11 January 2022.

6   Sinead Butler. *35 best Sue Gray memes as the nation waits for her Downing Street parties report to be published.* Indy1000, 27 January 2022.

7   Gareth Iacobucci. Eight hospital rebuilds are likely to be delayed beyond 2030, government says. *BMJ (Clinical Research Ed.)*, 381, 1210, 2023. https://doi.org/10.1136/bmj.p1210

8   David Waller and Rupert Younger, *The Reputation Game* (OneWorld, 2017), p. 143.

9   Salman Khan. Chief Reputation Officer (CRO): Envisioning the role. *Corporate Reputation Review*, 22(3), 75–88, 2019. https://doi.org/10.1057/s41299-019-00061-5

10 https://layoffs.fyi/

11 https://news.stanford.edu/stories/2022/12/explains-recent-tech-layoffs-worried

12 https://uk.pcmag.com/opinion/145812/women-are-hit-hardest-by-tech-layoffs

13 www.forbes.com/sites/emilsayegh/2024/08/19/the-great-tech-reset-unpacking-the-layoff-surge-of-2024/

14 www.mrmoneytv.com/post/are-stock-prices-affected-by-tech-layoffs

[15] www.businesstoday.in/technology/news/story/elon-musk-confirms-he -has-fired-over-80-of-twitter-employees-so-far-377045-2023-04-12

[16] www.theguardian.com/technology/2024/jan/02/x-twitter-stock-falls-elon-musk

[17] www.hubspot.com/company-news/a-message-from-hubspot-ceo-yamini-rangan

[18] https://oysterhr.notion.site/A-letter-from-Oyster-s-CEO-Tony-Jamous-43b7218897904211bf1486e314056d4e

[19] www.atlassian.com/blog/announcements/atlassian-team-update-march-2023

[20] Brené Brown. *Braving the Wilderness* (Random House, 2017), p. 107.

[21] www.youtube.com/watch?v=hDKJTOhtYiQ

Chapter 8: Building a relationship to manage reputation

[1] Michelle Ryan and Alexander Haslam. The glass cliff: Evidence that women are over-represented in precarious leadership positions. *British Journal of Management*, 16(2), 2006.

[2] https://fortune.com/2024/02/20/women-ceos-fortune-500-shorter-tenure-men/

[3] ibid.

[4] Gerald Ferris, et al. Relationships at work: Toward a multidimensional conceptualization of dyadic work relationships. *Journal of Management*, 35(6), 1379–403, 2009. https://doi.org/10.1177/0149206309344741

[5] ibid, p. 1385.

[6] ibid, p. 1389.

[7] ibid, p. 1395.

[8] Robert Liden, Smriti Anand and Prajya Vidyarthi. Dyadic relationships. *Annual Review of Organizational Psychology and Organizational Behavior*, 3, 139–66, 2016. https://doi.org/10.1146/annurev-orgpsych-041015-062452

[9] Geoffrey Love, Jaegoo Lim and Michael Bednar. The face of the firm: The influence of ceos on corporate reputation. *Academy of Management Journal*, 60(4), 1462–81, 2017. htttps://doi.org/10.5465/amj.2014.0862

[10] Jeffrey Pfeffer, *Power* (Harper Business, 2010), pp. 106–24.

[11] Roger Bolton, Don Stacks and Eliot Mizrachi. *The New Era of the CCO: The Essential Role of Communication in a Volatile World* (Business Expert Press, 2018). http://portal.igpublish.com.ezproxy-prd.bodleian.ox.ac.uk/iglibrary/obj/BEPB0000703

[12] ibid, p. 130.

[13] ibid, p. 80.

[14] Gerald Ferris, et al. Relationships at work: Toward a multidimensional conceptualization of dyadic work relationships. *Journal of Management*, 35(6), 1379–403, 2009. https://doi.org/10.1177/0149206309344741

[15] Robert Liden, Smriti Anand and Prajya Vidyarthi. Dyadic relationships. *Annual Review of Organizational Psychology and Organizational Behavior*, 3, 139–66, 2016. https://doi.org/10.1146/annurev-orgpsych-041015-062452

[16] ibid.

Chapter 9: Creating your reputation equity

[1] Benjamin Pfister, Manfred Schwaiger and Tobias Morath. Corporate reputation and the future cost of equity. *Business Research*, 13, 343–84, 2020. https://doi.org/10.1007/s40685-019-0092-8

Chapter 10: Reputation equity for non-CEOs

[1] Mary Ann Sieghart, *The Authority Gap* (Penguin, 2021), p. 109.

[2] ibid, p. 25.

[3] David Waller and Rupert Younger, *The Reputation Game* (OneWorld, 2017), p. 3.

[4] Frank Wolf, *The Narrative Age* (self published, 2024).

[5] https://narrativeinitiative.org/wp-content/uploads/2019/08/TowardNew Gravity-June2017.pdf

[6] https://en.wikipedia.org/wiki/South_Africa_national_rugby_union_team

[7] www.iol.co.za/mercury/opinion/springboks-a-metaphor-for-what-sa-could-become-d4743360-5029-4d05-ac0a-47dc397a5f69

[8] https://andyraskin.com/

Chapter 11: Reputation equity for founders – when you're both CEO and CCO

[1] https://www.stateofeuropeantech.com/ Report accessed November 2024.

[2] www.weforum.org/agenda/2024/03/women-startups-vc-funding/

[3] www.reuters.com/legal/us-court-decision-casts-shadow-diversity-venture-capital-funding-2024-07-02/

[4] ibid.

[5] www.africanews.com/2024/03/14/women-entrepreneurs-persistent-financial-obstacles-businessafrica//#:~:text=The%20entrepreneurial%20boom%20in%20Africa,to%20businesses%20led%20by%20women

[6] www.weforum.org/agenda/2024/03/women-startups-vc-funding/

[7] Yekaterina Kovaleva, et al. Becoming an entrepreneur: A study of factors with women from the tech sector. *Information and Software Technology*, 155, 107110, 2023.

[8] https://kellblog.com/2024/05/12/strategy-as-a-series-of-beliefs/

[9] www.personneltoday.com/hr/uk-businesses-join-consortium-to-recruit-ukrainian-refugees/#:~:text=A%20consortium%20of%20UK%20businesses,led%20by%20entrepreneur%20Emma%20Sinclair

[10] www.linkedin.com/posts/ecsinclair_where-possible-i-like-to-spend-both-enterprisealumni-activity-7175053099428904960-oGhx?utm_source=share&utm_medium=member_desktop

[11] www.neighbourly.com/blog/200-million-meals-donated-through-neighbourly

[12] Kim Scott, *Radical Candor* (Pan Macmillan, 2017), p. xvi.

[13] https://sifted.eu/articles/founder-linkedin-funding

Chapter 12: Towards new leaders

[1] Jeffrey Pfeffer, *Power* (Harper Business, 2010), p. 5.

[2] Kim Scott, *Radical Candor* (Pan Macmillan, 2017), p. 5.

[3] www.estherperel.com/blog/letters-from-esther-4

[4] www.mckinsey.com/featured-insights/mckinsey-explainers/what-is-leadership

[5] www.mckinsey.com/capabilities/people-and-organizational-performance/our-insights/the-inside-out-leadership-journey-how-personal-growth-creates-the-path-to-success

Bibliography

Barry Mitnick, John Mahon and Richard McGowan (2020) Reputation-sets. *Journal of Public Affairs*, 20(1), 2020. https://doi.org/10.1002/pa.2062

Benjamin Pfister, Manfred Schwaiger and Tobias Morath (2020) Corporate reputation and the future cost of equity. *Business Research*, 13, 343–84. https://doi.org/10.1007/s40685-019-0092-8

Bernard Bass (1990) From transactional to transformational leadership: Learning to share the vision. *Organizational Dynamics*, Winter 90.

Brené Brown (2017) *Braving the Wilderness*. Random House.

Charles Fombrun (1996) *Reputation: Realizing Value from the Corporate Image*. HBS Press.

Charles O'Reilly and Michael Tushman (2016) *Lead and Disrupt: How to solve the innovator's dilemma*. Stanford Business Books.

Danuta Szwajca (2018) Dilemmas of reputation risk management: Theoretical study. *Corporate Reputation Review*, 21(4), 165–78. https://doi.org/10.1057/s41299-018-0052-9

David Waller and Rupert Younger (2017) *The Reputation Game*. OneWorld.

Dominik Heil. Reputation Risk (2018) In Robert Heath and Winni Johansen (eds) *The International Encyclopedia of Strategic Communication* (pp. 1–6). Wiley. https://doi.org/10.1002/9781119010722.iesc0150

Frank Wolf (2024) *The Narrative Age*. Self published.

Gareth Iacobucci (2023) Eight hospital rebuilds are likely to be delayed beyond 2030, government says. *BMJ* (*Clinical Research Ed.*), 381, 1210. https://doi.org/10.1136/bmj.p1210

Gareth Morgan (2006) *Images of Organization*. Sage.

Geoffrey Love, Jaegoo Lim and Michael Bednar (2017) The face of the firm: The influence of ceos on corporate reputation. *Academy of Management Journal*, 60(4), 1462–81. https://doi.org/10.5465/amj.2014.0862

Gerald Ferris, et al. (2009) Relationships at work: Toward a multidimensional conceptualization of dyadic work relationships. *Journal of Management*, 35(6), 1379–403. https://doi.org/10.1177/01492063 09344741

Jeffrey Pfeffer (2010) *Power*. Harper Business.

John Blakey (n.d.) https://trustedexecutive.com/nine-habits-of-trust/resources-overview/

John Kay (2024) *The Corporation in the 21st Century*. Profile Books.

Kim Scott (2017) *Radical Candor*. Pan Macmillan.

Kovaleva et al. (2023) Becoming an entrepreneur: A study of factors with women from the tech sector. *Information and Software Technology*, 155, 107110.

Lauren Eaton, Todd Bridgmann and Stephen Cummings (2024) Advancing the democratization of work: A new intellectual history of transformational leadership theory. *Leadership*, 20(3), 125–43. https://doi.org/10.1177/17427150241232705

Mary Ann Sieghard (2021) *The Authority Gap*. Penguin Random House.

Michelle Ryan and Alexander Haslam (2005) The glass cliff: Evidence that women are over-represented in precarious leadership positions. *British Journal of Management*, 16(2).

Porter Braswell (2017) *Let Them See You*. Lorena Jones Books.

Priya Bates and Advita Patel (2023) *Building Inclusive Cultures*. Kogan Page.

Rachel Botsman (2017) *Who Can You Trust: How Technology Brought Us Together and Why It Might Drive Us Apart*. Public Affairs.

Rajeev Syal (2022) *Sue Gray: Who is official tasked with investigating No 10 party claims?* The Guardian, 11 January 2022.

Robert Eccles, Scott Newquist and Roland Schatz (2007) *Reputation and Its Risks*. Harvard Business Review. https://hbr.org/2007/02/reputation-and-its-risks

Robert Liden, Smriti Anand and Prajya (2016) Dyadic relationships. *Annual Review of Organizational Psychology and Organizational Behavior*, 3(139–66). https://doi.org/10.1146/annurev-orgpsych-041015-062452

Roger Bolton, Don Stacks and Eliot Mizrachi (2018) *The New Era of the CCO: The Essential Role of Communication in a Volatile World*. Business Expert Press. http://portal.igpublish.com.ezproxy-prd.bodleian.ox.ac.uk/iglibrary/obj/BEPB0000703

Salman Khan (2019) Chief Reputation Officer (CRO): Envisioning the role. *Corporate Reputation Review*, 22(3), 75–88. https://doi.org/10.1057/s41299-019-00061-5

Sinead Butler (2022) *35 best Sue Gray memes as the nation waits for her Downing Street parties report to be published*. Indy1000, 27 January.

Steven Boivie, Scott Graffin and Richard Gentry (2016) Understanding the direction, magnitude, and joint effects of reputation when multiple actors' reputations collide. *Academy of Management Journal*, 59(1), 188–206. https://doi.org/10.5465/amj.2014.0521

Tomas Chamorro-Premuzic (2019) *Why Do So Many Incompetent Men Become Leaders?* Harvard Business Review.

Waller and Younger (2017) *The Reputation Game*. OneWorld.

Zhong, et al. (2024) Workplace aggression and employee performance: A meta-analytic investigation of mediating mechanisms and cultural contingencies. *Journal of Applied Psychology*, 3 October, 2024.

Index

A

ABI Inform
achievements, highlighting 54
adaptation 88
advocacy 69
Alexander, John 43–45
Altria 102
Amazon 23, 105
ANC 8, 162
Ancell, Chris 88
apologizing, in a crisis 108–108
Arthur W. Page Society 121–122,
    129
Ashton, Antonia 154–155, 165
Atlassian 107
Atomico 167–168
authenticity 34–35, 70, 110, 163,
    185, *185*
  idea of, contested 36–37
authority building 172, 173–175
Axios-Harris Poll 100 78

B

barbeque test (Ettling) 97
Bates, Priya 37, 38
Bear, Meg 63–64, 67–70, 120, 147,
    149
behaviour(s)
  exclusionary 30–31
  four types of 181–182
  inclusive, top five 37
  non-CEOs 155–157
  and reputation 151
Bettencourt, Michele 90–91
bias 13
  avoiding 127, 137–138
Blakey, John 84, 118
Boeing 15

Böhringer, Martin 18–19
boys' club 27, 120
BP 87
Bradley, Kate 175
brand, use of term 94
Braswell, Porter 24–26, 27, 33–35,
    36, 37, 39, 53, 80–81, 82,
    171, 182
Fast Company 25, 172
Brewer, Roz 23
Bridgewater 34
Brown, Brené 113
Brown Duckett, Thasunda 23
B2B 149
building a relationship to manage
    reputation
  CCO remit and reporting line
    122
  CCO's trust building
    responsibilities 126–127, *129*
  CCO's responsibility: managing
    with intention 127–128
  CEO/CCO relationship, factors
    in 122–123
  CEO and CCO joint tasks in 119
  CEO's trust-building
    responsibilities 123–126, *129*
  coherence for target
    audiences 120–122
  importance, for leaders from
    diverse backgrounds
    116–117
  networks and power 120
  relationship between CEO and
    CCO 128–129, *129*
  working in a hierarchy 117–119
burnout 16
Business Search Ultimate 103

C

Cannon-Brookes, Mike 107
capability 103
CCGroup 82–83
Centre group 156
case studies
　the layoffs in tech 104–107
　leadership change comes from
　　within 180–182
　learning from a major reset
　　154–155
　the power of networks 158–160
　the Springboks – not just a
　　winning story, but a narrative
　　for a nation 162–163
Chamorro-Premuzic, Tomas 4,
　12–13
change management 88
character 20, 21, *21*, 88, 89, 103,
　118, 119, 120–121, 129–130,
　147, 186, *186*, 187
Chief Communications Officer
　(CCO)
　considerations for hiring
　　checklist 192
　joint tasks with CEO 119
　managing with intention
　　127–128
　objectivity 127
　questions for checklist 193–194
　relationship with CEO 122–123,
　　128–129, 128, 129
　remit and reporting line 122
　role of 103
　as reputation manager 115,
　　133–134, 185
　on reputation team 149
　and reputational risk 103–104
　speak truth to power 116
　trust building responsibilities
　　126–127, *129*
　use of term xix

Chief Executive Officer (CEO)
　change of, and communication 177
　considerations for hiring
　　checklist 191
　female, tenure of 116–117
　as founder, and communication
　　170–171
　and identity 48–49
　informal 71–72
　joint tasks with CCO 119
　knowing when and how to
　　approach 139–141
　matching their style 141
　neutral 65
　onus on 139
　questions for checklist 193
　relationship with CCO 122–123,
　　128–129, *129*
　and reputational risk 103–104
　role of 103
　startup, and reputation
　　management 175–176
　trust-building responsibilities
　　123–126, 128, 129
　see also understanding corporate
　　versus CEO reputation
Chief Human Resources Officer
　(CHRO) 125
　considerations for hiring
　　checklist 192
Chief Marketing Officer (CMO)
　125, 149
Chief Reputation Officer (CRO)
　103
Circuit Court of Appeals (US) 168
Citigroup 87, 88
coaching 65
Coco-Cola 19
cogs in the wheel 14–15
coherence 21, 21, *21*, 82, 89,
　120–121, 117, 133, 147, 177,
　186, *186*, 187

Colosimo, Zoe 174–175
communication
  bad news 20
  to build inclusive cultures 38–38
  and change of CEO 177
  identity and leadership 48–49
  and founders 185
  and layoffs 104–107, 177
  lean on your communicators
       185–186
  later-stage founders 171–172
  and location 176–177
  see also language and words
communication style 34–35
competitive advantage 82
competence 12, 20, 21, 21, 84, 87,
       88, 118, 119, 121, 123,
       129–130, 147, 186, 186, 187
conversations 81
corporate identity, redefining 102
Cotterill, Alayne Oriol 158–160
creative abrasion (Hill) 113, 138
crisis 119
  redefining 102
  what to do 107–108
crisis for leaders 12, 16, 17, 57, 81
crisis management see reputational
       risk and crisis management
crisis of leaders 12–13, 16, 57, 81
culture
  creating 59–62
  slow-burn change of 109–111
curiosity
  fostering 67–68

D
  Dadoo, Maya 98–99, 106
  Dalio, Ray 34
  Daw, Sara 156–157, 171
  Strategy and Leadership as Service
       171
de Stefani, Vania 99, 156, 163–164

Dickman, Amy 159
DEI (diversity, inclusion and
       equity)
  backlash against 26–24
  changing face of 24–26
  as multi-layered 26–31
diversity still matters
  activating inclusivity 31
  breaking taboos 31–33
  case study: navigating work with
       a perceived disability 28–29
  changing face of DEI 24–26
  communicating to build inclusive
       cultures 38–38
  DEI is multi-layered 26–31
  the facts 23–24
  insights: why the idea of
       authenticity is contested
       36–37
  thoughts for allies 38
  what unites these leaders 33–35
DoorDash 23
double-loop learning 70–71
dream job: keeping
  address microaggressions 66–67
  amplified emotional intelligence
       64
  appreciation for multiple
       perspectives 68–70
  creating the culture you can't see
       59–62
  don't rein yourself in 65–66
  foster curiosity 67–68
  investing in yourself 63–64
  lessons from senior leaders from
       diverse backgrounds 58
  non-linear can be the most direct
       route 58–59
  using informal communication
       71–72
  the value of neutral
       communication 65

dream job: landing or creating
  advice to emerging leaders 53–54
  finding leadership within 43–45
  identity, leadership and
    communication 48–49
  interrogate the leadership
    stereotype 42–43
  leading from outside the
    hierarchy 45–47
  lessons from emerging leaders 42
  non-linear, non-traditional, no
    fear 47–48
  not asking for permission 52–53
  use of language 49–52
dyads 117–119, 126

E
Eccles, Robert 76, 102
Edelman Trust Barometer 17
effective telling 98, 120, 175, 179
emotional intelligence 64
empathy 51, 52, 53
EnterpriseAlumni 173
European Accessibility Act (2025)
    30
exclusionary behaviours 30–31
executive communicator (EC), on
    reputation team 149–150
external reputational crisis 107–109

F
Farquhar, Scott 107
Fast Company (Braswell) 25, 172
Fearless Fund 168
feedback 51, 52, 117, 134–135
Ferris, Gerald 118–119, 123
Figge, Peter 152–153, 181
Finastra 124
Fombrun, Charles 76–77, 78,
    83–84
Football Foundation (FF) 47
Ford, Henry 15

Fortune 500 23, 78–79
founders
  and communication 185
  later-stage, and communication
    171–172
  layoffs 106
  reputation management 175–176
  see also reputation equity:
    founders
Fraser, Jane 87, 88, 115
FTSE Women Leaders Review 24

G
Gebhard, Liz 11–113
Gentry, Richard 91–92
glass ceiling 116
Google 23
Graffin, Scott 91–92
Frant, Adam 41
Gray, Sue 102
Great Disconnect 15
Gupta, Rishabh 50–51

H
Harris, Lou 78
Harris Fombrun Corporate
    Reputation Quotient (CRQ)
    model 78
Harris Interactive 78
The Harris Poll 78
Harvard Business Review 12, 25,
    102
Harvard Business School 113
Haslam, Alexander 116
head of communication
  role of 103
  use of term xix
hierarchy
  lack of diversity in 59
  leading from outside 45–47
  working in 117–119
Hill, Linda 113, 138

Holmes, Elizabeth 16
Home Depot 23
honesty 34–35, 43–44, 49, 84, 138
  feedback 117, 134–135
Hubspot 106

I
identity
  leadership and communication
    48–49
inclusion gap (Braswell) 25–26, 37
inclusive behaviours, top five 37
inclusive leaders 182–183
inclusivity
  activating 31
informal communication 71–72
information flow, managing 142–143
inside-out leadership 182
insights
  be fully human, not an archetype
    70–71
  investing in ways others don't
    have to 62–63
  the value of regular meetings 150
  why is the idea of authenticity
    contested? 36–34
internal reputational crisis 109–111
intersectionality 52–53

J
Jamous, Tony 89–90, 107, 153, 171,
    180–181
JodieAI 25, 33
John Deere 23
Johnson, Boris 102
Jones-Williams, Gillian 32–33,
    34–35, 39
Jopwell 25, 81, 172

K
Kau, Donald 134, 142–143
Kay, John 15

Koba, Katarzyna 170–171
Kolisi, Siya 162
Kolmetz, Katja 42–43, 49–50, 54,
    120, 170
Kovaleva, Yekaterina 168–169
Kyte Baby 19–20, 77

L
language and words 34–35, 65, 68,
    164
  in a crisis 108
  inclusive 182–183
  and inclusive cultures 38
  layoffs 106–107
  and meaning 134
  use of 49–52, 53
Lately.AI 175
layoffs
  case study 104–107
  and communication 177
  and language 106–107
  letters 106, 108
leaders
  emerging, advice to 53–54
  need for new 2–4
  reliance on old model 4
leaders from diverse backgrounds
  keeping dream jobs 58
  proactive reputation management
    97–98
  relationships and managing
    reputation 116–117
  reputational risk and crisis
    management 113
  use of term xix
  see also diverse leaders
leadership
  democratization of 71–72
  finding within 43–45
  identity and communication
    48–49
  inclusive 182–183

inside-out 182
non-linear, non-traditional 47–48
not asking for permission 52–53
redefining 183–184
transformational 16
use of language 49–52
use of term 41
leadership crisis
   crisis for leaders 12, 16, 17, 57, 81
   crisis of leaders 12–13, 16, 57, 81
   reputations at risk 18–20
   social media 17–18
   systems 14–16, 20
leadership stereotype, interrogating
   42–43
The Liberty Group 156
LinkedIn 37, 75, 90, 96, 157
Lion Landscapes 158
LMX 124, 126, 127
location, and communication
   176–177
Looney, Bernard 87, 101, 115
Love, Geoffrey 92
LUT, University of Finland
   168–169
Lyft 23

M
Mahon, John 102
Mandela, Nelson 162
Marinelli, Ernesto 64, 71, 82
McDonald's 19
M'Cwabeni, Vuyi 60–62, 65–66
McGowan, Richard 102
McKinsey Institute for Black
   Economic Mobility 23,
   181–182
meritocracy of ideas (Dalio) 34
messaging, planning 97
Meta 23
microaggressions 66–67
Microsoft 23, 105

Mitnick, Barry 102
Morgan, Gareth 14
Morris, Phillip 102
motherhood/parent tax 59, 62–63
motivation 110–111
Msema Culture 45, 170
Musk, Elon 105–106

N
narcissism 12–13
The Narrative Age (Wolf) 160
Narrative Institute 161
narrative moat (Wolf) 95, 104, 119
narratives 151, 160–161
Nath, David 51–52, 152, 164–165
needs, meeting 111–112
Neighbourly 174–175
Net Provider Score (NPS) 77
networks
   and power 120
   and reputation 151
   working on 157–158
neutral communication 65
Newquist, Scott 76, 102
Nielsen 78
Nolan, Paul 82–83
non-linear
   leadership 47–48
   as most direct route 58–59
non-traditional leadership 47–48
Nugent, Jack 152

O
Oxford University Centre for
   Corporate Reputation 17, 79
Oyster 89–90, 107, 153, 180–181

P
panic, in a crisis 107–108
Paris, Simon 124, 137, 139
Parker Review 26
Partygate scandal 102

Patel, Advita 37, 38
patriarchy 14
Pemberton, Tania 58, 62–63, 64, 65
perception 75
Perel, Esther 181
permission, not asking for 52–53
perspectives, multiple 68–70
Pfeffer, Jeffrey 70–71, 98, 120
portability 89–92
post-Covid hybrid working 30
power dynamics 117–119
preparedness 113
Pride Lion Conservation Alliance 158–160
privatizing 102
proactive reputation management 104, 119
psychopathy 12–13

Q
Quinn, Karen 140, 141

R
Race at Work 25
Rad, Jess 31–32, 36, 39
Rangan, Yamini 106
Raskin, Andy 163
reality distortion field, avoiding 137–138
Red Hat 23
reduction in force (RIF) 97
reparation, in a crisis 109
representation 49, 98–99
RepTrak model 78
reputation 53, 70, 71, 185
    aspects of 21
    aspirins and vitamins 93–94
    at risk 18–20
    and behaviours 151
    building your narrative moat 82
    CEO 87–100

character and competence 12, 20, 21, 21, 84, 87, 88, 103, 118, 119, 120–121, 123, 129–130, 147, 186, 186, 187
    is complex 76–77
    corporate 87–100
    goes two ways 79–81
    is hard to measure 78–79
    how identity helps 82–83
    inside-out 184–185
    is money 76
    personal 77
    and networks 151
    and social media 94–95
    and share price 87–88, 105, 115
    and stakeholder management 96–97
    trust, role of 83–84
    why it matters 75
reputation equity
    asking hard questions 135
    being intentional 138–139
    bias, avoiding 137–138
    CEO, being a soft space for 141–142
    CEO, knowing when and how to approach 139–141
    CEO, matching their style 141
    CEO, onus on 139
    echo chamber, avoiding 135–136
    hiring, what to look for 144
    honest feedback 134–135
    how to fix 143–144
    importance of 133–134
    information flow, managing 142–143
    reality distortion field, avoiding 137–138
    remembering who they serve 136–137
    when it all goes wrong 143

reputation equity: founders
  authority building 173–175
  communicating as a founder
    CEO 170–171
  how founders and startup CEOs
    manage reputation 175–176
  how later-stage founders
    communicate 171–172
  importance of 167–169
  when startups actively need
    communications advice
    176–177
reputation equity: non CEOs
  behaviour 155–157
  case study: learning from a major
    reset 154–155
  case study: the power of networks
    158–160
  case study: the Springboks – not
    just a winning story, but
    a narrative for a nation
    162–163
  find a coach 151
  importance of 147–149
  insights: value of regular
    meetings 150
  knowing your unique identity
    152–154
  knowing yourself 152
  language 163–164
  mistakes to avoid 150
  narratives 160–161
  reputational tools 151
  who is in your reputational team
    149–150
  work on your networks 157–158
Reputation Institute 78
reputation management 20,
    95–96
  CCO's role 115, 127–128,
    133–134, 185
  CEO's role, startups 175–176

importance of 97–98
reputational risk and crisis
    management
  case study: The layoffs in tech
    104–107
  CEO and CCO work together on
    103–104
  external reputational crisis
    107–109
  internal crisis 109–111
  learn from vulnerability 111–113
  managing 136–137
  vulnerability, factors in 102
  what academics say 101–103
  what leaders of diverse identities
    can learn 113
reputational team 149–150
reputational tools 151
results, quarterly pursuit of 15
Rise 33
Rise, Mzansi 8
risk of risks (Szwajca) 101, 104,
    105–106
Robert, Musema 45–47, 49, 170
RoboKoba 170
Russell Reynolds and Associates 116
Ryan, Michelle 116

S
SAIC 23
Schatz, Roland 76, 102
Scott, Kim 16, 176, 181
Seed funding 167–168
SensiVR Health 171
share price, and reputation 87–88,
    105, 115
shareholder value 15
Sharma, Shuchi 37–38
Shetty, Preeti 47–49, 157
Sieghart, Mary Ann 13, 148
Sinclair, Emma 173–174
Sinclair, Neil 173

Sinek, Simon 41
single-loop learning 70–71
Sirius/XM 175
Snap 23
social media 76-77, 92, 179, 185
  and leadership crisis 17–18
  and reputation 94–95
Sonnenfeld, Jeffrey 19
space 123–126, 128
spin 19–20
The Springboks 162–163
Staffbase 18–19, 81
The Stagwell Group 78
stakeholder management 96–97
Starbucks 19
stick and carrot approach 16
storytelling 47, 160, 161, 185
Strategy and Leadership as Service
    (Daw) 171
systemic problems 14–16, 20
Szwajca, Danuta 77, 101, 104

T
taboos, breaking 31–33
team cohesion 113
Tesla 23
TIAA 23
time 123–126, 128
Townes-Whitley, Toni 23
transformational leadership 16
transparency, in a crisis 109
True Search 25
trust 17, 83–84, 109, 117–119, 123,
    179
2045 Studio 25, 26, 33

U
UN Sustainable Development
    Goals 180
understanding corporate versus
    CEO reputation
  aspirin and vitamins 93–94

having a voice 99
how CEO reputation affects
    company reputation 89
how CEOs talk about reputation
    92–93
portability 89–92
proactive reputation management
    95–96
representation matters 98–99
the role of social media 94–95
stakeholder management 96–97
why proactive reputation
    management matters for
    diverse leaders 97–98
underrepresented minorities
    (URM), use of term xix
unicorn startup, use of term 180
Upshot 47, 157

V
Valle, Margherita Della 24
value, externalizing 54, 120, 179
Vaux, Angie 26, 33–35, 39, 120
Vodafone 24
voice, having 99
von Matt, Jung 152
von Riel, Cees 78
vulnerability
  exercise run 111
  learning from 111–113

W
Walgreens 23
Waller, David 79–80, 88, 89, 94, 151
Wavemakers 43, 46, 170
Wayfair 23
Wolf, Frank 81, 82, 95, *161*
  The Narrative Age 160
The Womanhood 32
Women in Tech forum 26–27
workplace pairs 117–119, 126
Worky 98–99, 106

X
X 105–106

Y
Yale Chief Executive Leadership
    Institute 19
Younger, Rupert 19, 79–80, 88, 89,
    94, 151

Z
Zibi, Songezo 8
Zoom 23

A quick word from Practical Inspiration Publishing...

We hope you found this book both practical and inspiring – that's what we aim for with every book we publish.

We publish titles on topics ranging from leadership, entrepreneurship, HR and marketing to self-development and wellbeing.

Find details of all our books at: www.practicalinspiration.com

Did you know...

We can offer discounts on bulk sales of all our titles – ideal if you want to use them for training purposes, corporate giveaways or simply because you feel these ideas deserve to be shared with your network.

We can even produce bespoke versions of our books, for example with your organization's logo and/or a tailored foreword.

To discuss further, contact us on info@practicalinspiration.com.

Got an idea for a business book?

We may be able to help. Find out more about publishing in partnership with us at: bit.ly/PIpublishing.

Follow us on social media...

@PIPTalking

@pip_talking

@practicalinspiration

@piptalking

Practical Inspiration Publishing